CO-CREATING GOOD, HEALTHY RELATIONSHIPS

Living Life "The WeWay" With Everyone, Every Day

BY

WENDY J FOXWORTH

This book contains stories in which the author has changed people's names and some details of their situations to protect their privacy.

Cover art direction and infinity graphic by Multi Channel Marketing, Albuquerque, New Mexico.

Published by the Center for Consciousness Education
Albuquerque, New Mexico 87107
ISBN: 0615902138
ISBN 13: 9780615902135

Recommendation

"Co-Creating Good, Healthy Relationships:
Living Life " The WeWay" With
Everyone, Every Day *by Wendy Foxworth comes
out of a deeply experiential and dedicated explo-
ration of our human potential to move beyond
self-centered relationships into true partnership
with ourselves, others and our Earth community.
We are given clear roadmaps to put us on "The
WeWay" and to help us go further than we thought
possible. A gift for the future of humanity!"*

-Victoria Friedman, Co-Founder, Vistar Foundation
Dedicated to Collective Evolutionary Consciousness

Table of Contents

Dedication

Every person who has the privilege to incarnate as a human being on this planet is here for a definitive and divine reason. Each person plays his or her role in evolving the consciousness of life. Each person serves in a place on the continuum of consciousness where his or her energy serves to lift themselves and others up to advanced levels of understanding and growth for the benefit of all life forms.

The human being through whose consciousness this book was written is one whose entire life has been devoted to learning about and creating pathways to realize unconditional love, respect, and trust in human relationships. This book is dedicated to the principle of unconditional love and the realization of that unconditional love in the context of human relationships.

It is intended as a call for all who would identify themselves as world servers to realize unconditional and positive regard for all human beings so that peaceful co-creation can become a lived reality. It is the intention of this book to provide frameworks about relational patterning and interaction agreement templates that show people how unconditional love can be lived - right now - in the midst of all relationships.

Acknowledgments

Deep gratitude is extended to the following individuals who played a pivotal role in the revelation of the ideas presented in this book:

- Donald Laurin and Mary Lou Foxworth for being my parents and providing sustenance, education, and the example of how telling the truth works to create the deepest of loves, even when it hurts sometimes.

- My sisters, Deborah, Beth, and Cindy, and my brother, Gary, for putting up with my inventive, creative, and adventuresome nature as a sibling.

- To all the teachers/friends/spouses/co-workers/coaches/ churches/clients who provided the education, prayer, financial support, and pregnant wombs of relationship through which the ideas presented in this book were revealed: Mr. Monroe, Lori Furse, Doug Schaffer, Cheryl Erbes, Marian Sanders, Rev. Louis De Spain, Rev. Jim Harris, Donna Lockridge, Meleese Seigler, Rev. Ken Martin, Rev. Sherre Boothman, Ravi Verma, the denomination of Metropolitan Community Churches (especially churches located in Albuquerque, New Mexico; North Hollywood, California; Austin, Texas; St. Louis, Missouri; Kansas City, Missouri, and Orlando, Florida), Rev. Elder

Troy Perry, Rev. Brent Hawkes, Rev. Elder Nancy Wilson, Rev. Elder Lillie Brock, Rev. Judy Dahl, Rev. Teena Carpenter, Rev. Phyllis Hunt, Rev. Denis Moore, Rev. Kurt Krieger, Rev. John Barbone, Rev. John Middleton, Rev. Jim Merritt, Donna Thomas, Kathy Janes, Linda Davidge, Louise Raimondi, Rev. Leslie Heyboer, Pam Connor, Polly Davis, Mary Manin Morrissey, Barbara Marx Hubbard, Gary Zukav, Jean Houston, the Society for the Universal Human, the Living Enrichment Center, all the people and practitioners of Inner Light Ministries, Rev. Deborah Johnson, Valerie Joi Fiddmont, John F. Kennedy University Masters in Management Program, Nancy Southern, Lloyd Williams, the entire Getz family, Rev. Patrick Pollard, the board of directors, and congregation of the Center for Spiritual Living in Albuquerque, New Mexico, Sally Parker, and the Center for Consciousness Education, a 501c3 charitable organization that has dared to stay true to doing things according to their **We**Way, which they call "a culture of collaboration, co-creation and cooperative relationships".

- To all those who provided professional editing and agenting services I give my deepest gratitude. I especially am grateful for the genius of support provided by Brian Palmer, Michael E. Browning, Paula Getz, and the design team at CreateSpace.

Most importantly, I want to express deep and everlasting gratitude to the love of my life, my wife, Paula Getz, whose constant devotion, commitment, and support of living life according to our **We**Way agreement at home and at work continues to fortify my resolve to share this learning worldwide. The "we" that Paula and I are together is the most meaningful and treasured part of my life, and I look forward to all that the future will bring through our daring to do relationship differently. Thank you, Paula, for being on this adventure with me to remove obstacles to love in this world.

May all who read these words be blessed and better supported in making unconditional love a reality on this planet.

Author's Statement and Caveat

In the face of my frustration at what was my family's version of dysfunction (*Me*Way) a question arose in my five-year-old mind, "Where is the love I came here to experience?"

It's not that there was no love present, but the experience and knowing of love was fleeting and intermittent. As with all spiritual qualities, love is eternally present. Yet living love in-body and particularly between-bodies has been a huge challenge for everyone, including myself. It seemed from those small eyes that love was what everyone was trying to get through how they chose to interact with others. Yet no matter how hard we all tried, love seemed to be more elusive and hard to get.

The *struggle* to love? Something was definitely wrong with the collective picture.

It became my passion early in my life to live love into reality. I wanted the deep peace, joy, and creativity that showed up for me when love was present. The good news is that I have lived and loved in many different relationships and failed miserably in some of them. The *even better* news is that because of failing so often, and admitting it, I was led to the dawning of an incredible revelation. How I was interacting with other people, and how we all tend to interact with each other as human beings is blocking our capacity to be the love we really are.

The exciting and *best of all* news is that if we are willing to do what it takes to change our interaction pattern so that it is aligned with the universal spiritual quality of love, then the love that we really are will reveal itself and be our collective experience!

Imagine with me the great delight of finding out that the suffering we experience in our relationships is totally optional. After you finish this book you will know that suffering, pain, and the agony of relational disharmony and violence are simply the consequence of choices regarding how we interact with each other.

Specifically, what was revealed to me through my life experience was the fundamental truth that relational suffering was the outcome of a specific pattern of relational interaction that I call the *Me*Way. The *Me*Way is how we "do" relationship when we are ego-invested or ego-identified. Some common *Me*Way expressions are: "I love you if you *do it my way*", "It's all about *me and my kind*", and "It's *my way or the highway*".

I believe it was the *Me*Way that Jesus had in mind when on the cross he said, "Forgive them, for they know not what they do."

Of absolute amazement to me was the realization that the *Me*Way only results in one thing: separation of relationship. The *Me*Way creates a huge block for anyone who desires to know love's presence. The *Me*Way results in our participating in daily acts of unconscious relational violence toward one another physically, mentally, emotionally, and spiritually. The *Me*Way is fear-based, and our investment in it is all about self-interest and the survival of the ego/body.

This *Me*Way pattern of interaction is universally present wherever human beings are found. This pattern is exhibited in different forms of relationship in all human societies regardless of nationality, race, sexual orientation, age, language, gender, or any other category of difference. Interacting in a *Me*Way results in divorce, child abuse, job firings and resignations, broken homes, systemic oppression of minority groups, homophobia, racism, crime, genocide, terrorism, poverty, hunger, illness, and disease. The *Me*Way interaction pattern is what blocks our awareness and ability to realize unconditional love for humanity and in our relationship to our beloved planet earth.

The most challenging aspect of the revelation of the *Me*Way was the realization that no individuals by themselves have the capacity to change this pattern of interaction. One can't order up or impose unconditional love. For unconditional love to become a reality and to stop being a participant in contributing to relational violence (doing things the *Me*Way) in our world, we must find at least one other human being who is able to live intentionally in a **We**Way relational interaction pattern. To change our pattern of interaction requires being in a conscious and intentional relationship with people who choose to live in a **We**Way.

It is helpful to readers to know where the *Me*Way and the **We**Way fits in terms of the evolution of human consciousness. Readers should refer to the Map of the Scale of Consciousness on page xxvi in David Hawkins's book *Truth Versus Falsehood: How to Tell the Difference*. This book addresses issues of primary concern for people who suspect that they are making a shift in consciousness from the level of the 400s to the 500s on the scale. The essential shift involved in moving from a *Me*Way of being to a **We**Way of being involves using the intellect of the 400s in service to the leanings of the heart in the 500s.

Using the framework of the **We**Way will bring you to the threshold of the door of unconditional love at the 540 level of consciousness. Crossing the threshold means making the choice to live in a **We**Way in every relationship in your life.

Not everyone is capable of making a shift from a *Me*Way to a **We**Way of being due to their current level of consciousness, and this simply needs to be accepted. The truth is we are all evolving and we are where we are in consciousness until we are ready to shift to the next stage of consciousness.

Thus, it would be appropriate for people whose are in the stage of consciousness that calibrates at 499 or less to understand the **We**Way as a sort of pipe dream and probably a totally unrealistic strategy for human relationship. In actuality, the **We**Way *is* a utopian nightmare for anyone's ego. People who are strongly ego-identified do not yet have the capacity to care about or honor the wisdom of others. Because of this they will resist any movement of a relationship or organization toward implementing a **We**Way of being.

In the **We**Way there are no ladders of success to climb, no competition, no person more or less important than anyone else. There is no one to rule over and no one who knows it all. There are no victims. There is only the **We**Way and how each individual contributes to its realization.

When we live in a **We**Way we know we are all in it together. We know deep in our bones that we have never "done" life alone or by ourselves. There isn't a human being alive who isn't supported by an incredible matrix of relationships.

The ego doesn't have the capacity to believe that togetherness or a **We**Way is possible. Nor does the ego believe that it is important to consider the feelings and thoughts of others, because the ego is "I" not "We" focused. The egocentric person is constantly skeptical and resentful about issues of love, respect, and trust. He or she knows that if the ego truly seeks love, respect, and trust, it won't be able to continue its perpetrator/victim dance and the drama of creating separation in his or her relationships. Accepting responsibility for its part in creating separation is not a skill of the ego. For this reason, a *Me*Way person will typically do everything he or she can to keep people focused on accomplishing tasks - getting the work done and having no time for relationship. Emotional availability for relationships with others is practically nil.

Essentially, to live in a **We**Way requires a readiness to yield individuality (ego/personality/individual preferences) in service to the collective wisdom of all those involved in a relationship. At times it requires yielding to the collective voice of the "we" of our spousal relationships or family. At other times it requires yielding to the collective voice of a work team or an organization that we either work for or serve as a volunteer. At other times it requires yielding to the collective voice of the entire human race and planet earth.

In essence, to make the shift from a *Me*Way to a **We**Way requires a yielding of the individual to the collective of whom he or she is a part - one of the many voices that makes up a whole. The shift requires yielding the personal, individual, and particular (ego/small self) to the collective, interpersonal, and universal (Self). The **We**Way is essentially a methodology that supports people in learning how to understand, abide by, to live in the context of - and in relationship to - collective versus individual/egoic wisdom.

The decision to live in a **We**Way is not a frivolous one. Stepping into the **We**Way is to make a choice to leave the *Me*Way world behind. It is a life-changing experience that will literally turn your life upside down and inside out. You will be literally transformed and catapulted into a new dimension of being.

WeWay people commonly believe in a power greater than themselves. This higher power has many names. **We**Way people can most often be found in inclusive community/spiritual support groups, New Thought/ Ancient Wisdom communities, twelve-step programs, and businesses that have sustainable, earth-friendly practices. It is very important that these groups welcome everyone regardless of personal differences. If a group proclaims a particular spiritual path, it is important for the group to acknowledge that its path is only one of many valid and valuable spiritual paths available. There are some inclusive spiritual communities in all faith traditions, as well as independent churches formed to provide the kind of support needed by **We**Way people. There are also coaches, counselors, spiritual directors, and other spiritual/recovery support groups that can fill the supportive community role.

This community support is important as you make a shift in relational interaction patterning, because it is not uncommon to feel a bit crazy and even lonely temporarily when you begin to live in a **We**Way. The new way of being is not familiar to you and many other people. The feeling of being crazy happens because even though you are in the process of making the shift, up to 80 percent of the world's population is still unconsciously addicted to living the conventional *Me*Way. Only 20 percent of people in the world will be able to relate to the change you are making. As regards people who can't relate to the **We**Way, remember it isn't personal. With great compassion, you will need to accept that 80 percent of the world's population does not yet have the capacity in consciousness to understand the principles and interaction patterning described in this book.

It can feel immensely intimidating to dare to live life differently. Just as a recovering alcoholic needs other alcoholics to heal and recover, so too do **We**Way people need people like themselves. As those in recovery from any addiction learn, one often has to find new friends, new jobs, and sometimes even new family in order to learn how to stop the addictive behavior. Healing into the **We**Way from the *Me*Way is no different.

The foundation of the **We**Way is profoundly and deeply spiritual, but not religious. You can live the **We**Way without going to church. The intent of the **We**Way is to support the realization of the innate human capacity to be unconditional love in the everyday affairs of human relating. To make the shift to interact in a **We**Way, it is important to wholeheartedly and without reservation commit yourself to realizing oneness, connection, unconditional love, and relational harmony with your fellow human beings. This commitment to these spiritual qualities is what will attract all the resources needed to live abundantly in this still predominantly *Me*Way world. You must be ready and willing to put principles before personalities.

The ideas revealed in this book also can serve as a bridge for people making the shift from the first to second tier of consciousness as described in the book *Spiral Dynamics*. Authors Don Beck and Christopher Cohen state that, "the most significant marker of the exiting green stage (*first tier of consciousness*) into the yellow stage (*second tier of consciousness*) is the dropping away of fear. Life is life, after all. Tribal safety, raw power, salvation for all eternity, individual success, and the need to be accepted diminish in importance. Instead, there is a growing curiosity about just being alive in an expansive universe. The person realizes how incredibly much there is to know and explore while accepting his or her finite life. One begins to look at the group objectively, yet with concern. There is no deliberate rejection of belonging, but the need to be a part of something is fading. Bigger issues appear on the horizon that are beyond the scope of any community to handle within itself. A very different kind of thinking is about to emerge as the yellow meme awakens the second tier of human existence."

The things you will learn in this book will confront any remaining vestiges of unfinished ego work that may be blocking your capacity of unconditional love and thus living in second-tier conscious relationships. The *even better* **We**Way is a framework that describes ways of thinking and interacting necessary for the ego/self to live into the soul/Self in its relationships with other human beings. The **We**Way provides tracks to run on that eventually lead to the threshold of the door through which you step into unconditional love.

The truth spoken in these pages cannot be proven except by personal experience. There is no way to measure the probability of anyone's success. Every **We**Way experience is radically inter-subjective and dependent on the stage of consciousness and collective decisions of the people who make up the relationship or organization. The **We**Way is simply one methodology or pathway that can lead you to experience unconditional love - *if you have the commitment to do what is needed to live it into your daily life.*

More succinctly, the **We**Way works when "WE" work it!

I believe that all readers of this book are pioneers in evolutionary consciousness, and together we are making the world a more loving place. May the ideas in this book do nothing other than bring a brighter light, love, and hope to your everyday experience.

Wendy Foxworth, MML
October 19, 2013
Albuquerque, New Mexico, USA

Preface

"*If you don't have a consensus that it is nonsense - you don't have a breakthrough.*"

-BRUCE RATTAN

"*We need thousands of people, starting with ourselves, to come out of the trance of the small self. To quiet our mind through meditation so we are fully present in the timeless now; to step back from the collective trance of consuming and devouring the earth in order to try to fill the void within ourselves, which can never be filled from the outside and to take steps to get off the grid, to reduce our fossil fuel emissions - to work to have our governments and corporations reduce fossil fuel emissions, to conserve energy, to preserve wild habitats, to seek to love each other; to make peace with everyone in our lives and most of all, because we can't do it without ourselves, to make peace and treat ourselves with compassion.*"

-DR. CRAIG F. SCHINDLER

"*You never change things by fighting the existing reality. To change something, build a new model that makes the existing model obsolete.*"

-R. BUCKMINSTER FULLER

The new model of relational interaction described in this book provides practical ideas for co-creating a future that works for everyone and our planet. We create our reality by how we choose to interact as we attempt to fulfill our personal and collective visions as members of the human race. It matters not where we live in this world. We are inextricably bound up and interconnected in a matrix of human relations through which our reality is created each and every day.

Life doesn't happen to us, it happens through us and our daily relational interactions with each other. We are creating heaven or we are creating hell. It is all up to us.

Despite all the ways we keep trying to kill each other off because of our differences, we are one race and one people. We are one in being human and are in the process of evolving into an even greater and more promising future. As Barbara Marx Hubbard states so succinctly in her book *Emergence*, we are at a "choicepoint" regarding our future evolution. The question before us is whether we evolve consciously and intentionally for the good of all or choose to evolve through revolution where a few people will continue to benefit at the expense of the many. So far we seem to consistently choose revolution as our collective response to life's challenges. It is time to realize that in spite of all our talk about the need for peace, our revolutionary actions and interactions continue to create war. We have to become conscious of the fact that every day our most common patterns of interaction result in our experiencing either love or fear, peace or war.

We are powerful as human beings. Our everyday interactions with other members of the human race are literally responsible for creating life or death, love or fear, peace or war, progress or decline. We are made in the image of the creator of the universe (by whatever name we each may or may not ascribe to that creator) and thus we have power that can be used to support life or destroy it.

The big illusion we've been swimming in is that someone other than ourselves is responsible for what we experience in this world. The truth is that we are all fish swimming in the same tank of water. We are all equally responsible for creating the condition of the water our lives depend on. No one fish or one entire species of fish has the power to change the condition of the water. We are all dependent on the same water for our individual and collective well-being, so it would be good for us to stop blaming someone else for what will always be a shared creation. We never do anything alone. Everything is a group creation for which we are responsible. Even the gods of many names won't save us from our co-creativity. It is we who will save ourselves or not by the choices we make in our creations.

All of us are responsible for the manifestation of terrorism being acted out in our world today. We keep distracting ourselves from our collective responsibility by pinning blame for our pain on the Hitlers, Husseins, Christians, Jews, Muslims, parents, children, men, women, black people, white people, heterosexuals, homosexuals, poor people, and rich people. The blame game has never and will never work to solve our collective problems. We fail to see that no amount of blaming or killing any individual or group of individuals will stop the terrorism and continued acts of relational violence we continue to co-create in our relationships with each other.

Terrorism is the direct result of a system of beliefs and assumptions that drives us to interact in ways that can do nothing but increase our experience of relational violence toward each other. This system of beliefs and relational interaction could be called the "Me" Way. The only way to end the terrorism of the *Me*Way is to intentionally develop a new shared understanding of a system of beliefs and assumptions that will drive us to interact in ways that produce peace and harmony in our relationships worldwide.

The good news is that this new system of beliefs and relational interaction - the "We" Way - is being birthed in many forms around the globe. Many members of the human race can no longer tolerate the pain of the *Me*Way and are dedicating themselves to a new way of interacting with their fellow human beings. In the past fifteen years a surge of people has been opting out of the "us versus them" game and getting people with different perspectives but common interests together to create solutions to problems affecting the entire human race.

A prime example of this is the work being done by the Irish singer and humanitarian Bono in getting world leaders to work together to end global poverty. Bono has learned the art of facilitating **We**Way agreements, and the entire human race is benefiting because of his dedication to finding and focusing on these shared agreements.

Another glowing example is the Gates Foundation. Bill and Melinda Gates of computer software company Microsoft are using more and more of their wealth to create **We**Way alliances with politicians all over the world to meet the most pressing education and health needs of the human race. Together, they cross all boundaries to bring people to the same table to create workable solutions for everyone.

Yet a third example is the partnership of former presidents and rivals George H.W. Bush and Bill Clinton. Moving beyond their political pasts and likely present political disagreements, both men came together and raised millions of dollars to help people harmed by the Indonesian tsunami of 2004 and Hurricane Katrina in the United States.

We learn more about the shared wisdom of all of us when we pool our resources and knowledge and the value of needing to let go of our sides on issues to create new solutions that are good for all of us. This is the heart of the **We**Way of doing life.

This book reveals the "Way of We" that is being birthed into our world and provides the steps anyone can take to make a conscious shift out of the *Me*Way and into the **We**Way.

Introduction

All successful life ventures are accomplished through the interaction of human beings in relationship with one another. You can have the most heartfelt desire to live in loving relationship with a life partner or the most daring organizational vision, yet fail simply due to how people actually interact with one another. The inability of people to interact in productive ways, whether personally, socially, or professionally, has a tremendous negative impact on us as a people, and planet earth as a whole. Immense amounts of time, money, and energy are lost because we continue to have great difficulty in our relationships with each other.

After twenty years of consulting with organizations, teaching organizational development, and coaching organizational leaders and committed couples, it has become clear to me that how we interact within relationships and organizations needs to change. We need to create a pattern of interaction that enables us to nurture, develop, and sustain healthy, productive personal and professional relationships.

The work of Jean A. Hollands, in her book *Red Ink Behaviors: Measure the High Cost of Problem Behaviors in Valuable Employees*, spells out the immense loss of time and money an organization absorbs when its members are unable to work well with others. This book provides a model for setting up patterns of interaction that will enable any form of organization - couples, families, spiritual communities, corporations, and governments - to live harmoniously.

Chapter 1 is a very basic primer on organizational/relational development. The focus in this chapter is on the critical effect patterns of relational interaction have on people in any organization. The people affected by these patterns of interaction will act in ways that positively or negatively affect the organization's or the relationship's ability to fulfill the reason it exists and to experience positive and productive growth as a result of its efforts.

Chapter 2 describes our typical pattern of interaction as human beings - the *Me*Way. The *Me*Way is the foundation of all relational violence. If we interact in the *Me*Way, the only outcome will be the repetitive experience of separation in our relationships.

The result of interacting the *Me*Way creates your personal experiences of betrayal, abuse, cheating, conflict, assault, battery, murder, adultery, codependency, addictions, dysfunctional family relationships, and divorce. Interacting in the *Me*Way creates the workplace experiences of forced resignation, sexual harassment, job demotion, inequitable compensation plans, workplace conflict, decreased productivity, and declining revenues. The *Me*Way interaction pattern results in worldwide human experiences of poverty, human oppression of all kinds, terrorism, ethnic cleansing, genocide, environmental degradation, and war.

The good news is that we have the power as human beings to change our pattern of relational interaction to co-create a world where we live in harmony and peace and profit personally and collectively as a result. Harmonious personal and working relationships can be a reality if we collectively pledge to heal from our *Me*Ways and choose instead to interact in a way that results in the nurturing and sustaining of relationships of mutual respect for all people.

Living life the "**We**Way" is introduced in Chapter 3. The **We**Way pattern of interaction provides a template for a way of relating that focuses on co-creation and collaboration instead of the comparison and competition required to interact in the *Me*Way.

Chapter 4 describes what is required for people to make a shift from *Me*Way relating to **We**Way relating. Suggested steps for this shift are made for people involved in committed primary relationships, people in the workplace, and people in spiritual communities.

The **We**Way is catching on worldwide. It is being lived out more and more in human communities all over the world. Thousands of books, seminars, and workshops exist; more are being created every day that help people to move into the **We**Way of "doing" relationships. Chapter 5 is devoted to identifying other authors, programs, concepts, and ideas that are working to help people move toward increasing their capacity to live in the **We**Way.

It is a given that the **We**Way cannot be accomplished alone. It only works in a relationship between two or more people willing to design and implement a written agreement that spells out ways they will act that are in alignment with their unique **We**Way.

The **We**Way is dependent on the work of a new wave of people known as world servers. These world servers are rising up, offering solutions to lower levels of relational stress and anxiety so that a stable peace can become a reality for all members of the human race. It is the intent of the **We**Way to partner with all world servers in supporting and furthering their individual contributions to a lived peace that is profitable and beneficial for all people and for our planet.

We continue to collect examples of the **We**Way being lived out in different ways and in all forms of human relationship. People reading this book are encouraged to give feedback on the ideas in this book and make us aware of others doing this work worldwide so we can provide clients working examples in their local communities. If you would like to learn more about the **We**Way and how to introduce it to your family, friends, neighbors, and co-workers, please visit our website at www.theweway.com.

We have much work to do and the time is ripe! Thank you for taking the time to learn about the **We**Way. You are invited to join us as together we co-create a positive and life-giving future for our people and our planet.

Wendy J. Foxworth, MML
Albuquerque, New Mexico, USA
October 19, 2013

Chapter 1: Organizational Development 101

A human organization consists of two or more people working through their relational interactions to create specific outcomes. Based on this definition, two people in a spousal relationship or two friends or two co-workers in relationship are forms of human organization. Wherever we are in relationship with another human being, we are in an organization, co-creating outcomes through our interpersonal interactions.

In human organization, we are in relationship to accomplish something that cannot be achieved by one of us alone. In essence, we cannot accomplish it alone but can do so through our interaction with each other. On a daily basis we are all participants in multiple forms of human organization. At one time we can be a spouse, a parent, a child, a sibling, an employee, an employer, a member of a spiritual community, a stockholder, a mentor, and a friend. In every form of human organization we co-create what we believe about ourselves and then attempt to interact behaviorally in ways aligned with what we believe.

Every form of human organization has a culture that significantly impacts the organization's ability to achieve its outcome or fulfill its purpose. An organization's culture consists of three primary components that together work synergistically to enable members to accomplish and fulfill their reason for existing.

As seen in Diagram 1.1, the vertical and primary dimension of an organizational culture is the *context* of the organization. The context is usually described in the organization's guiding documents. For profit and nonprofit businesses, those guiding documents come in the form of vision, mission, or charter statements. Another document fairly common these days is a statement of values. The context of a culture reflects a shared agreement of organizational members regarding the core principles, values, and the "big picture" goals of what is to be achieved. The context tells others why the organization exists. The context of most business transactions involves a contract that begins with a purpose statement.

Diagram 1.1

Organizational Culture

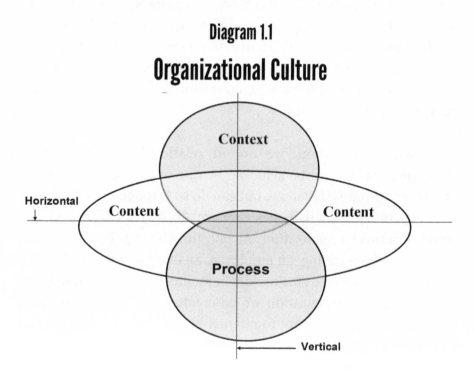

Interpersonal relationships with life partners, for example, have pre-nuptial agreements, marriage licenses, relationship vows, and other forms of commitment agreements. Broadly speaking, in all forms of human organization our context states who we are and why we exist.

The second component of an organization involves the *processes* used to live in alignment with the context of that organization. All actions taken in an organization are processes that take place through the vehicle of relational interactions between members of the organization. Processes involve human beings interacting in certain patterns of behavior that fulfill the vision of the organization. The pattern of interaction for people in committed relationships with spouses - whether married or not - will result in their feeling connected or separated. In essence, we are successful or not in fulfilling our reason for existing as an organization or relationship based on how we choose to interact with each other.

In attempting to live in alignment with our context (principles, values, and "big picture" goals) we have all experienced interacting in beneficial and non-beneficial ways in our relationships with other people. The key point here is that if we are going to co-create world peace, successfully attain our goals, or a long-term relationship, it will happen through establishing a pattern of relational interaction that accomplishes our shared context.

The third component of an organizational culture is *content* (see Diagram 1.1). The content of an organization includes the services or products offered and the structures (job descriptions, roles, financial resources, etc.) that enable the members of the organization to deliver the services. The content of any organization will change to fulfill its context at different points in time. Some examples of content changes in the workplace are personnel changes, resource availability, and work processes. The content of a co-worker or spousal relationship involves individual interests, activities, beliefs, assumptions, and the roles people play to get the work done.

In my work as an organizational and relationship consultant, once the context (vision-values) is set, I find that most of us file the context in the deep recesses of our minds. It is easiest for all of us to decide on the content. At work, we get most excited about deciding what services we will offer or what structures we will create to deliver the services most efficiently and effectively. In a personal relationship, we quickly forget our wedding vows or commitments made to one another and get focused on caring for the house/body, going to work, eating, sleeping, recreating, community activities, or paying the bills. Many of us easily spend up to 95% of everyday focused on content issues of the organization or our relationships.

What is most challenging in every organization and relationship, is establishing the relational process component through which everything we do manifests or comes to be. Whether we like it or not, everything happens through our interactions with each other in every arena of our lives. I saw a greeting card once that asked the question, "Why does life have to be so complicated?" The answer inside said, "Oh yeah...people are involved."

Life doesn't happen to us. Life happens *through* our interactions.

Working with people to accomplish shared goals is much easier said than done. Though intuitively we all know our collective success as a human race is dependent on experiencing harmonious relations with other people, this component of our organizations or relationships is usually given the least attention.

We pay incredible attention to bettering the performance of individuals at work, particularly our leaders and their ability to motivate or empower workers on the front line. Married partners pay great attention to how each partner is or isn't meeting their individual needs. However, there is little attention paid to the interactions between people that either empower or disempower members of any relationship to realize their shared dreams and goals.

Wendy J. Foxworth

In my work as a mediator and Relation-Shift Coach, I find that conflict situations are rarely about the issue(s) presented. People in the conflict resolution business frequently have similar experiences. The real issue in these situations is usually how people experience the interactions between themselves and others as they attempt to find a solution. Most conflict happens because people don't feel that their relationship or organizational partner is interacting with them in a way that supports them to relate in a cooperative manner. Conversely, most conflict is resolved when the parties are able to come to an agreement about how they will interact in the future so that cooperative action is possible.

Relations between people, not situations, block shared goal accomplishment. Thus, making changes in the pattern of interactions between people is required if goal accomplishment is to be achieved. If a production goal at work isn't being achieved, the people involved in achieving the goal will need to change how they interact with one another. If spouses are unable to solve a particular issue, they will need to change how they interact with one another in order to find a solution. New outcomes become a possibility when we are willing to change how we relate to each other.

We can have the grandest visions of what we want to accomplish, and yet those visions will only be accomplished through how we choose to relate with each other. As you will learn in the rest of this book, goal accomplishment and productivity in human organizations are dependent on successfully making the shift from *Me*Way to **We**Way patterns of relating.

Chapter 2: The MeWay

The *Me*Way is a pattern of relational interaction that has been lived out in human relationships for a very, very long time. This behavior pattern has served as the "norm" for our interactions in our families, workplaces, local communities, countries, and international relationships. We are so used to relating in a *Me*Way that it has become automatic for us.

Here are three examples of living life the *Me*Way:

MeWay Example 1: Sherry and Sam at Home

Sherry's friend calls and invites her and her husband, Sam, to a weekend party. Sherry tells her friend that she and Sam will be there. Sherry tells her husband they are going to a party on Saturday afternoon. He resents that Sherry didn't talk to him before she made the commitment. Instead of telling her about his resentment, he complies with her request. As the weekend approaches, Sam is distant and quiet. He works late and doesn't come home on time for dinner. When Sherry asks what is wrong he tells her he doesn't want to go to the party. Sherry says he has no option because she has already said yes. Sam feels powerless to change the decision. Sherry kisses him, but he doesn't kiss back. He calls his golf buddies and gripes about Sherry and the decision she made for him, which will cut his game short tomorrow.

On Saturday morning, Sam plays golf with his friends and has a great time. He loses track of what time it is and gets home late. Sherry is upset and rushes him to get ready and out the door to the party. They don't say a word to each other all the way to the party. Neither of them has a good time at the party. Sherry gets home and calls her friend to apologize for being late and tells her friend it was Sam's fault. Sam tells Sherry he's going to the bar for a few drinks with the boys.

MeWay Example 2: Working with Julie

Julie has just been promoted to the director of her department at work. She has hired her new team and has set up a team training session with an outside consultant approved by her boss. While going through her e-mail she is shocked to read that her boss has been promoted to a vice president position and that the president has appointed a new person to be her boss. Julie will get to interview the so-called potential new boss, whose name is Joe. However, she is told that Joe will be her new boss no matter what because the president of the corporation hand-picked him. Joe is hired and becomes Julie's boss. Joe doesn't like Julie's ideas about her department and tells her that the money won't be there for the outside consultant. He tells Julie what to do and how to do it. Julie resents that she isn't consulted regarding projects she is familiar with. Joe is hard to contact. He is slow to answer e-mails and return phone calls.

Julie feels powerless to change the situation, yet knows it isn't right. Because Joe won't listen to her, she spends a lot of time on the phone with her co-workers and team members, who also don't like Joe's work habits. They all talk about how to get rid of Joe because of his horrible people skills and are looking for jobs outside of the company. Julie begins showing up at work late and unprepared. She frequently takes sick days due to back pain. Little work is accomplished. Revenues are down and the quarter profits are slowed considerably. Joe is under pressure to perform and blames Julie and his other direct reports for these results. Julie, her co-workers, and team members blame Joe for the low quarterly numbers. They are all doing their own thing without communicating with others while wondering what will happen next.

MeWay Example 3: Pastor and the Board of Directors

Attendance at church services has been low and financial giving is decreasing. The board of directors has done nothing to get ready for the annual stewardship drive that is scheduled to begin in two weeks. The pastor is anxious, as there isn't enough money to make budget. She resents that the president of the board is doing nothing about it. The pastor goes to a seminar, where she learns about a new stewardship program. When she comes home she tells the board of directors about the new idea. Most of the board members are pleased the pastor took the lead on this and agree to use the new program. One board member says she would like to compare programs before the decision is made. In response, the pastor tells the board there is no time to compare programs, and that this has to be done at this time of the year or it will mess up the annual plan of ministry action the congregation approved. Even though she already works seventy hours a week completing her duties, the pastor commits herself and the church administrator to prepare all the material so they can kick off the giving campaign as scheduled in two weeks. The board votes unanimously for the pastor to go ahead.

The pastor ends up doing all the work and desperately needs help to complete the project. The board members are too busy to help. The pastor's spouse is angry that the pastor has no time for their relationship and asks for a divorce. The relational stress and anxiety increases to the point where the pastor has a heart attack. The congregation blames the board for not doing their job and adding to the pastor's workload. Board members leave the church and the pastor resigns. The congregation of 350 people slips to an all-time low of 78 members. The congregation has to sell its building and can only afford a part-time pastor.

Each of the three examples shows a repeated pattern of *Me*Way behavior as seen in Diagrams 2.1 and 2.2 on the following pages.

Diagram 2.1

MeWay Culture of Command and Control

This diagram shows how relationship partners get goals accomplished.

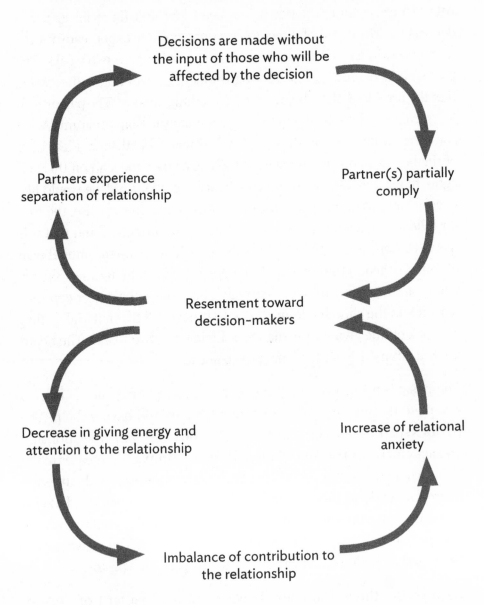

Decisions are made without the input of those who will be affected by the decision

Partner(s) partially comply

Partners experience separation of relationship

Resentment toward decision-makers

Increase of relational anxiety

Decrease in giving energy and attention to the relationship

Imbalance of contribution to the relationship

Wendy J. Foxworth

Diagram 2.2

MeWay Culture of Blaming Relationships

This diagram shows how relationship partners manage relational anxiety and handle differences of perspectives about issues.

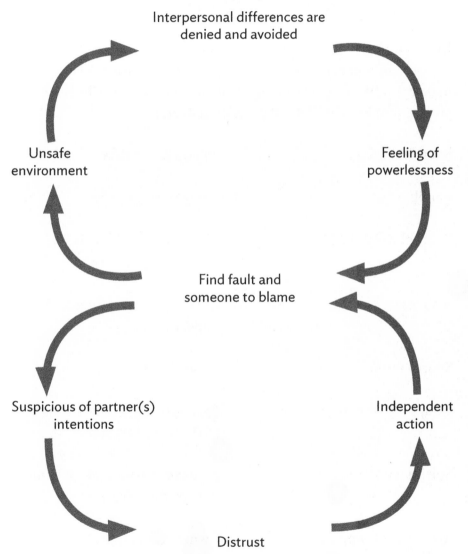

Interpersonal differences are denied and avoided

Unsafe environment

Feeling of powerlessness

Find fault and someone to blame

Suspicious of partner(s) intentions

Independent action

Distrust

Diagram 2.1 describes the *command and control* nature of how work gets done according to the *Me*Way. Diagram 2.2 describes the *blaming* nature of how differences of opinion are handled in the *Me*Way. The top loop of each diagram represents the basic pattern of behavior. The bottom loop represents the consequence of people repeatedly acting out the top loop behaviors in their interactions.

In Diagram 2.1, the command and control behavior of the *Me*Way is initiated by someone who makes a unilateral decision. The decision maker can be one person or a small group of people. The list below gives examples of unilateral decision makers:

Form of Relationship	Unilateral Decision Maker
Family	Parents or Guardians
Spousal Relationship	Either Spouse (usually the biggest money-earner)
Business	CEO, Directors, Managers or Supervisors
Sports Team	Head Coach
Nonprofit Organization	Executive Director and Board of Directors/Trustees
Spiritual Community	Minister/Pastor and/or Board of Directors/Trustees
Apartment Complex	Owner and Manager
Government	President, Governor, Mayor, City Councils

A unilateral decision is one made without input from those affected by it. It is the common assumption of *Me*Way decision makers that they know best and are qualified based on their personal understanding alone to make decisions that are good for everyone involved. *Unilateral decision making* was evident in all three example situations:

1) Sherry made a decision for Sam based on her schedule and her desire to go to her friend's party,

2) The president of the company hand-picked Julie's boss,

3) The pastor decided for the board what stewardship program would be used.

In the second step of the loop in Diagram 2.1, the decision makers tell others about their decision. They expect others to comply with their decision. In our example situations:

1) Sherry expected Sam to go to the party,

2) The president expected Julie to work with Joe,

3) The pastor expected board members to go along with her idea.

When the decisions were communicated to those affected by them, they all complied, even though they were upset about not being consulted prior to the decision making process. Sam went to the party. Julie attempted to work with Joe. The board members went along with the pastor.

In *Me*Way organizations the partners believe they have no other choice but to *comply with the decision makers*. Sam complied with

Sherry because he knew Sherry would gripe and complain for weeks if he didn't go. Julie complied with the president's choice because she feared losing her job if she questioned his decision. Even though church board members wanted to compare other programs, they complied with the pastor's suggestion because they felt guilty that they hadn't fulfilled their responsibilities.

Because the partners' opinions are not considered in decision making, *the partners resent the decision-makers.* As a result of their resentment, the partners distance themselves from the decision makers and resort to sabotaging projects through withdrawal or withholding of information, or they simply resign or leave the relationship, which is the ultimate consequence of the unilateral decision making process.

As depicted in the bottom loop of Diagram 2.1, the price we pay for doing things the *Me*Way is *huge.* Once the partners become resentful (top of the bottom loop), they respond by *decreasing their level of participation in the relationship or organization.*

This part of the relational interaction loop is demonstrated in our example situations where:

1) Sam worked late, withheld kisses, played golf, was late for the party, and chose to go drinking with the boys instead of being with Sherry,

2) Instead of doing her work, Julie spent her work time trying to get rid of the new boss and find a new job,

3) As the pastor worked overtime to fulfill the board's responsibilities, the overload of tension and anxiety triggered the psychosomatic event of a heart attack that landed her in the hospital.

The *increase in relational stress and anxiety* resulted in the experience of a broken relationship.

The *Me*Way is a lose/lose proposition in the long run. Sherry could divorce her husband. The company could keep replacing employees. The congregation could elect new board members and hire new pastors. In each case the investment that all parties made in their relationship is lost. Everyone has to start anew to rebuild the relationships necessary to accomplish the relationship or organizational goals. The turnover costs for *Me*Way behavior are significant, usually denied, and rarely measured.

The *Me*Way Command and Control culture is strengthened to create increasing levels of anxiety and resentment between people because of an underlying *Me*Way Blaming Relationship culture, as seen in Diagram 2.2.

The blaming relationship nature of *Me*Way relationships and organizations happens because there is *no place for different perspectives to be shared, valued, and validated*. In fact, different opinions and perspectives are avoided. Everyone is expected to hold to the party line or the "status quo" as dictated by the unilateral decision makers. Because there is no process by which differences are heard, *partners feel powerless* about being true to what they uniquely have to offer.

Both the partners and the decision makers *take the victim position and find fault in others*. The decision makers look for someone to blame for why their decision isn't working, and partners claim personal duress due to the decisions made by the decision makers.

Sam blames Sherry for messing up his weekend. Sherry blames Sam for messing up her plans. Julie blames the president and her new boss for making her life miserable. Joe blames Julie for his poor quarterly report. The board blames the pastor for agreeing to the stewardship campaign. The congregation blames the board for not doing their job and caring for their pastor.

Notice that the blame game doesn't solve the issues for anyone in these three scenarios. No one feels safe and no one wants to be the one who gets blamed.

The bottom loop of Diagram 2.2 illustrates that once the partners and decision makers start finding fault and blaming each other, they begin to *assume that bad intentions exist toward one another*. People can actually act paranoid and believe that others are out to get them. Distrust is prevalent, causing everyone to act independently. There is no cooperative action.

The chaos caused by independent action and the increased workload on the decision makers only fuels their justification to make more unilateral decisions. Literally, they don't think they have the time to do anything but make unilateral decisions, and in taking that action the organization begins to experience another cycle of command, control, and blaming behavior.

You would think these types of experiences would make us see that not including people in the decision making process contributes to our collective detriment. Yet in the *Me*Way, the unilateral decision has to stand, and there is no room for different opinions. When things go wrong we don't look for alternative solutions. Instead, we ignore all differences of opinion, even if one of them is ours. We suppress our differences and those of others. We *"go along to get along" or "agree to disagree"* - or so we say.

In all three examples, the unilateral decision makers - Sherry, Julie's boss, the president of the company, and the pastor - assumed the people for whom the decision was made would agree with them. People on whom such decisions are imposed are expected to comply, and usually they do. However, they resent the decision makers because they had no input.

If this way of making decisions happens repeatedly, *people begin to respond by leaving the relationship.* In the case of a committed spousal relationship, one of the spouses asks for a separation or divorce, has an affair with someone else, or the couple live as roommates and cease being lovers. In the case of an employer/employee relationship, the employee may find another job or stay in the job but actually work less than 50 percent of the time at the job for which he or she is being paid. In spiritual communities, members sabotage forward progress by withdrawing financial giving or reducing their participation.

Author Jean Hollands calls *Me*Way behavior *"Red Ink Behavior"* in her book *Red Ink Behaviors: Measure the Surprisingly High Cost of Problem Behaviors in Valuable Employees.* The core idea of her book is that negative employees cost money. Jean and other members of the Growth and Leadership Center in Mountain View, California, created a "costimator" which estimates the cost of an employee exhibiting problem behaviors. In her book, she provides a quick checklist of red ink behaviors. All of the red ink behaviors are typical *Me*Way behaviors. A person who interacts using red ink or *Me*Way behaviors:

- Attacks others or benign situations

- Creates barriers between people

- Inhibits productive dialogue

- Avoids conflict or accelerates conflict without resolution

- Does not use consensus as a decision making strategy

- Contradictory in conversations

- Takes credit even when not due to his or her efforts

- Creates chaos and crisis

- Criticizes people in public

- Lobbies for own perception without hearing others' points of view

- Dictates decisions

- Evasive when data or action is required

- Does not give or receive feedback constructively

- Doesn't easily adapt to changes in directions

- Humorless

- Inhibits creativity

- Inability to motivate others

- Does not listen

- Organizationally scattered

- Politically naïve

- Impulsive and reactionary

- Unable to accurately define his or her effect on others

- Does not seek feedback

- Reluctant to share knowledge, teach others or participate interactively

- Can't mend difficult situations

- Resistant to new ideas

- Does not stay open to options

- Uses sarcasm that puts others on guard and evokes distrust

- Does not maintain visionary understanding or big picture planning

- Unable to engender or experience trust with others

- Withholds information

The cost of these behaviors is immense. Each has a negative effect on the capacity of a relationship or an organization to fulfill its purpose. However, what the *Me*Way interaction patterns described in Diagrams 2.1 and 2.2 reveal is that these behaviors are never done in isolation. They arise because of deeper relational interaction patterns present in our human relationships. We exhibit negative behaviors, creating separation and distrust, because of how we unconsciously interact with each other.

We are deeply mistaken if we think we can get rid of these negative behaviors by getting rid of someone with whom we are in relationship. People fire people and divorce each other every day, only to find themselves in another job or relationship in which these same behaviors recur. All individual behaviors are a part of a pattern of relational interaction.

Until all parties agree to interact differently and change their pattern of relational interactions, negative "Red Ink" behaviors will still appear in the organization or relationship. Healing negative *Me*Way behaviors requires organizational members and relationship partners to be co-creative in naming and describing the interaction pattern of behaviors they are willing to be accountable to in co-creating a **We**Way future.

What is important to notice about the *Me*Way pattern of behavior is that it is only created through the interaction of at least two or more people. No person alone can create a shift in a pattern of behavior that takes at least two people to create. All patterns are co-created through interactions with other people. If we don't like the *Me*Way pattern of behavior, it will require the agreement of those involved in the relationship or organization to make a shift in the relational patterning so a **We**Way pattern of behavior can emerge.

Chapter 3: The WeWay

"Two hundred years from now in the 23rd century, historians will look back at our era as the Great Awakening. They will say that an inclusive movement in which millions of people took responsibility to live with love and respect for each other and all life was able in the 21st century to create peace on earth. They will say this Great Awakening was preceded by a dark time when human actions threatened life on earth. Many called it a spiritual revolution because at its heart was both the individual awakening to the light of the soul and the dawn of our conscious humanity. Future historians will note that this interfaith, multi-faith, environmental movement had its roots in earlier movements for spiritual development and human potential, for civil rights and women's rights, for the environment, for social justice, for peace. This movement developed methods for personal healing and inner peace, and for dialog and conflict resolution so people of different points of view could listen to each other and work together for common goals."

-DR. CRAIG F. SCHINDLER

The **We**Way is a pattern of interaction that has been rising up in different forms since at least 1950. It is relatively new on planet earth, and people frequently are skeptical about its capacity to manifest in human affairs. It is often what people describe when they answer the question about designing their perfect relationship at home with family or at work with co-workers or with people they are in relationship with in spiritual communities or other community-based organizations. Many people have encountered this pattern of interaction intermittently in our *Me*Way world of today and crave the experience.

Here are three examples of living life the **We**Way.

WeWay Example 1: Jack and Jill at Home

Jack and Jill's wedding vows contained their shared values of love, respect, trust, integrity, and relational harmony. They pledged to base their relationship on living these values no matter what was going on in their lives. Their commitment to each other wasn't tied to circumstances that would change over time, such as their levels of income, job titles, children, family members, spiritual traditions, activities, and interests, where they lived, or what social causes they supported. Their promise was to respond to all life situations from their shared perspective about who they felt called to be in the world. They decided that who they were, both as individuals and as a couple, was of greater value than achievements or any material or financial assets they might accumulate.

Together they co-created a ***Relational Interaction Agreement*** that described how they would relate with each other in a manner consistent with their values (see Appendix A for an example of such an agreement). They understood that all arenas of life - called the ***8 Spheres of Relational Wholeness*** in ***The WeWay Relational Development System***© (physical, emotional, intellectual, relational, spiritual, moral, values, and self-identity) - are opportunities to live in alignment with their shared values.

Whenever a decision was needed, Jack and Jill used their values as the criteria by which they made their choice. For instance, when Jack was presented with the option of a promotion at work that would require moving to another state, the question Jack and Jill asked themselves was,

"How will relocating to another city and having increased job responsibilities, along with increased financial resources, affect our ability to manifest love, respect, trust, integrity, and relational harmony in our relationship?"

In a dialogue, Jack and Jill shared their different perspectives about the new opportunity. They spent a long time looking at the benefits of the new job, yet in the end decided to decline the promotion. They decided against it because moving would decrease their capacity to sustain meaningful connections in their relationships with their friends, families, and their spiritual community. Additionally, Jack knew that the leadership style of his new supervisor was top-down, which wouldn't support him in creating trusting and respectful relationships with his co-workers. Taking the promotion would lessen Jack and Jill's ability to live in alignment with their values, and no amount of money was worth losing their individual and collective integrity.

WeWay Example 2: Working with Jane

Jane had a passion to help create a collaborative culture in the corporate arena that would enable all employees to have more balanced lives and more meaningful work experiences. She decided to start sharing her dream with a few other people to see if there was any interest in creating a new vision for corporate America.

It was at this time that Jane's friend, Tom, turned her on to a **Relation-Shift Coach** who helped her see that her problem wasn't upper management or the good ol' boys network. She saw how the command and control corporate structure was the outcome of a belief system that resulted in a pattern of relational interaction. No one was at fault. Everyone was playing a role in keeping the pattern in place, including Jane.

Jane saw how blaming upper management for being the problem was a fundamental aspect of the company's command, control, and blaming culture. She realized that unless some core beliefs (and the resulting pattern of behavior) changed, the company's results would not change. She learned that she could be a part of shifting that interaction to a pattern that would support cooperative relationships instead of competitive ones. Instead of looking to upper management to make this shift happen, she decided to hire her coach to help design a game plan for her department to make the shift in relational interaction patterns. Jane chose to be the change she desired.

To support leadership development for departmental employees, Jane asked the corporation to hire her coach to perform a department assessment of relational interaction patterns. The results of that assessment were then fed back to the entire department. Department members self-assessed the organization as having a command, control, and blaming pattern of interaction. It was the desire of everyone in the department to shift to a collaborative, co-creative, and cooperative relationship culture. Jane's coach facilitated the co-creation of a **Relational Interaction Agreement**, a new department charter, and department goal statement.

After only six months of using their **Relational Interaction Agreement**, miracles happened. Because department members had a shared agreement, the playing field was leveled. Everyone in the department was evaluated based on whether he or she did their work in alignment with the shared agreement. All work plans were co-created by department members. The "us versus them" game plan disappeared. Department members were now willing to do more than their job to complete a project. Individual work plans included having adequate sleep and time to be with family. The workday was limited to eight hours for all department members. Everyone was expected to participate in at least one community social betterment project.

Department members met once a quarter to evaluate their shared agreement and to make any needed revisions. Each person evaluated themselves on how they were living up to the agreement, and made amends and/or gave accolades to fellow department members for moving through their most difficult interactions. Asking for forgiveness and making requests for do-overs to realign with doing things in alignment with the agreement became common place. Everyone learned that respect and care for one's co-workers means saying you are sorry - a lot - especially in the first six to twelve months of living according to the shared agreement. By practicing the agreed upon behaviors every day, the department eventually became known as the best place to work in the company.

At the last check-in, department members gave Jane a special gift to thank her for the risks she had taken to be a different kind of leader. They laughed about their own initial skepticism toward what they called a "touchy-feely" relational agreement and the significant amount of time it took to get it together in the beginning. They remarked that this was the most meaningful work experience of their lives. It was so good to be treated well and cared about as a whole human being, not just someone who put in time doing a job.

As of the last report, Jane was receiving commendations from corporate vice presidents and departmental coordinators. In a worldwide assessment of departmental activity, Jane's staff received the highest level of achievement. The president of the company requested Jane to be the plenary speaker about the benefits of creating a collaborative culture in the corporation.

WeWay Example 3: Reverend Peter and the Board of Directors

Reverend Peter was recently called to serve as minister at a church that had experienced three church splits over different issues in the past ten years. He accepted the call with the understanding that the church would participate in an all-church assessment to discover what had caused the splits in the past and to co-create a plan of action to avoid future ones.

The board of directors hired a **Relation-Shift Coach** to conduct a church assessment. The assessment was conversation-based and all questions were open-ended. Interviews were conducted with all paid and volunteer leaders. Focus groups were conducted to receive input from different sub-groups in the church. All congregational members were invited to give their input in writing. Everyone was asked the same fifteen questions.

A thematic analysis was performed on the assessment question responses. The following revelations were discovered:

1) The church's splits were caused by three different issues

2) People expressed their disappointment and hurt regarding how those in leader positions treated them

disrespectfully and in unloving ways during the time preceding each split

3) People were concerned about finding a way to interact in loving ways so that everyone would stay and get involved in active ministry in the church

4) People felt the church's vision, values, and ministry plans reflected those of only a minority and not the whole congregation

The **Relation-Shift Coach** delivered the assessment results to the congregation in the context of an all-day seminar about church development. The coach taught church members about command, control, and blaming relationship cultures and collaborative, co-creative, and cooperative relationship cultures. Members were amazed to see how the different cultures affected their ability to live out the love Jesus lived and taught about in the Bible.

The members and leaders of the church realized that to live love in their relationships with one another they needed to change their organizational culture. They woke up to the fact that enduring loving relationships can't be lived out in what members and leaders agreed was the *Me*Way command, control, and blaming relationship culture of their past and that all this culture did was create relationships of separation or some form of a church split.

There was unanimous agreement that nothing save a conscious and intentional movement toward creating a culture of collaboration, co-creation, and cooperative relationships would work to keep them from experiencing yet another church split in the future.

The congregation agreed that their first step was to create three guiding documents:

1) An agreement of relational interaction to spell out the congregation's shared principles and values and how they would interact so that those principles and values were evident in every action they took

2) A vision statement

3) A ministry plan of action statement

The second step was to embed the new culture into all aspects of the life of the congregation, including, but not limited to, the infrastructure of staffing, the music program, meeting agendas, leadership training, membership classes, worship, educational events, budgeting, and building use. Until their guiding documents could be created, those present agreed to abide by a sample agreement of relational interaction provided by the coach.

The congregation was excited about creating their shared vision, and just having those who attended the seminar live according to the agreement brought a new spirit of lightness and love into relationships between people in the church. The focus of all church activity now is to see a resulting increase in people's capacity to love one another. The word is getting out, and already attendance is increasing and people are stepping up to get involved in being of service to others.

In all three **We**Way situations described above there is a repeated pattern of behavior as depicted below in Diagrams 3.1 and 3.2.

Diagram 3.1

WeWay Culture of Collaboration and Co-Creation

This diagram shows how relationship partners get goals accomplished.

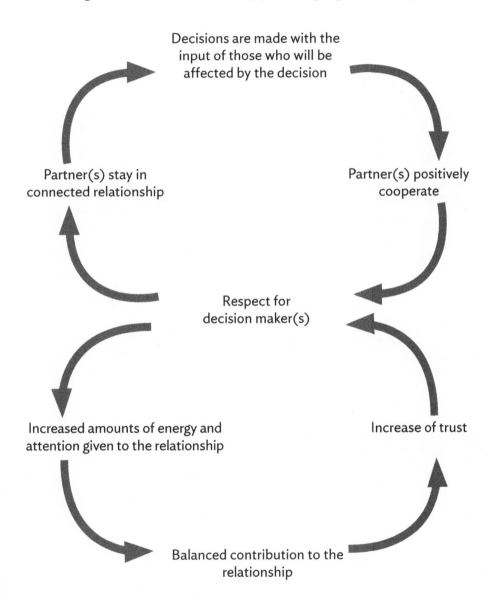

Decisions are made with the input of those who will be affected by the decision

Partner(s) stay in connected relationship

Partner(s) positively cooperate

Respect for decision maker(s)

Increased amounts of energy and attention given to the relationship

Increase of trust

Balanced contribution to the relationship

Diagram 3.2

WeWay Culture of Cooperative Relationships

This diagram shows how relationship partners manage relational anxiety and differences of perspectives about issues

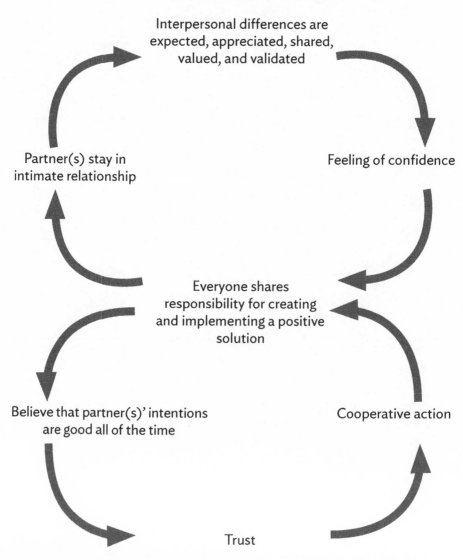

Interpersonal differences are expected, appreciated, shared, valued, and validated

Feeling of confidence

Partner(s) stay in intimate relationship

Everyone shares responsibility for creating and implementing a positive solution

Believe that partner(s)' intentions are good all of the time

Cooperative action

Trust

Wendy J. Foxworth

Diagram 3.1 describes the *collaborative and co-creative* nature of how work gets done in a **We**Way organization or relationship. Diagram 3.2 illustrates the *cooperative* nature of the relational interaction that enables people to live collaboratively and co-creatively. The top loop of each diagram represents the basic pattern of behavior, and the bottom loop represents the consequences of top loop behaviors.

In Diagram 3.1, the collaborative and co-creative behavior of the **We**Way is initiated by someone who takes into consideration the thoughts and feelings of others as they contemplate making a decision regarding a particular issue. **We**Way decision makers still have the responsibility to make a decision, but before they do, they solicit the input of those who will be affected.

There are two core beliefs in a **We**Way organization or relationship:

Everything anyone does affects other people.
Results achieved always happen through
interactions between two or more people.

Because the interaction between people is the channel through which any outcome is created, it is deemed pertinent to take the thoughts and feelings of those who will be affected into consideration before a decision is made. If people's input is taken into account before decisions are made, the decision makers not only have the best information possible to consider, they will also reap the positive cooperation of those who will implement the decision.

This doesn't mean that every person in the organization has to give input about every issue on the table. Some people will be more directly affected than others depending on the issue.

Regardless of the presenting issue, the first step a **We**Way decision maker takes is to assess who needs to give input and acquire that input before deciding anything. A team leader doesn't sit in his or her office and decide what order to issue to enact a solution he or she prefers. For the most part, once couples have a *Relational Interaction Agreement*, or organizations have their guiding documents, people are free to be creative in how they go about accomplishing tasks in ways that are in alignment with the shared agreements in their areas of responsibility. However, all **We**Way decisions are made based on the collective input received for the good of everyone involved in the organization or relationship.

The decision makers in **We**Way and *Me*Way relationships and organizations are the same people. The only difference is how they go about making their decisions (see Appendix E, *The WeWay 10 Step Decision Making Process*).

As a rule of thumb, once the guiding documents are collaboratively created and agreed upon in **We**Way relationships and organizations, all members are free to fulfill their responsibilities without interference by others. The guiding documents create alignment of relational interaction expectations that are clear and behavior specific, so there is little room for misunderstanding about how those involved agree to interact as they accomplish their shared goals. As a result, because of the consistency of a **We**Way relational experience on a day-to-day basis, anxiety remains at low levels while people expand their capacity to trust each other and experience the freedom to be true to themselves in the midst of the relationship.

WeWay spouses love to be in each other's presence no matter what house they live in, what job they have, or how much money is in the bank account. They know they are appreciated for who they are and that they are in a relationship with a partner who will be with them through the good and bad times no matter the circumstances. Employees get excited about being in a workplace where their unique perspectives are valued and where they can know meaningful and caring relationships as they accomplish their goals. People show up and are creative in ways never thought possible when things are done the **We**Way.

On a day-to-day basis, **We**Way relationship partners and organizational members abide by the relational agreement in how they conduct themselves. When decision makers adhere to their **We**Way agreements, people respect them and actively support the implementation of their decisions.

This respect is evident in Jack and Jill's relationship, because in turning the job down, Jack chose to honor his relational agreement with Jill. Respect for Jane by her staff members and other company leaders quadrupled because she initiated the creation of a relational agreement and then lived in alignment with that agreement. Reverend Peter was highly respected for his willingness to help the congregation define in their own words what would enable them to love one another, and by doing so he avoided another church split. He could have insisted that they fulfill his vision for the church, but instead he showed them that he was there to serve the shared vision of the congregation and willing to ascertain its shared agreement.

As can be expected, once respect is present in a relationship or an organization, people increase the amount of energy and attention they are willing to give to it. There is a mutuality of participation in getting the work of the relationship or the organization done, creating a more balanced contribution and workload for everyone involved. Because everyone in the relationship or organization knows they are in this **We**Way relationship together, they can trust others and are trusted by others.

Jack and Jill's experience of intimacy continually deepens. Both partners appreciate one another, and their commitment to living in integrity with their shared values grows more important each and every day. Whereas Jane's staff hardly put in four hours of work a day before they created their agreement, they now put in at least eight hours. Staff morale and esteem are at an all-time high. Productivity and profits are up. People feel good about being at work. There isn't anything these staff members wouldn't do for Jane today. She now has a home life and actually has time to spend building relationship with her significant other.

When people attend Reverend Peter's church, they remark upon how loving people are toward each other. Because of their **We**Way *Relational Interaction Agreement*, members know they have a voice that matters and that they are making a difference in the lives of people in their community. Clergy and lay leaders familiar with Reverend Peter's church regularly send teams from their own churches to learn how to create a **We**Way culture.

Living in a **We**Way relationship or organization is a win/win proposition. As can be seen on the left side of the top loop in Diagram 3.1, the deep respect and trust present between people means that not only do they stay, but they tell others about how great it is to be a part of the relationship or organization. Jack and Jill always speak about each other with great appreciation and praise in ways many other couples can only yearn for. Jane and members of the department speak only positively and constructively about their relationships and tell people that their department is the best department in the company to work in. Members of the congregation Reverend Peter serves wouldn't dream of being part of another church. Relationship anxiety and drama are minimal in all three forms of relationship/organization. Work gets accomplished without sacrificing the individual and collective genius of everyone involved in the relationship or organization.

In a **We**Way relationship or organization we are all in this together - it is our primary experience every day. **We**Way relationships have *Black Ink Behaviors*, which are essentially the opposite of what Jean Hollands describes as *Red Ink Behaviors*. Positive home and work relationships are the means to achieving good for the triple bottom line of people, planet, and profit. Men and women who interact in and work in **We**Way organizations and relationships exhibit the following *Black Ink Behaviors*:

- Authenticity and credibility

- Competency

- Awareness of his or her impact on other people

- Supports people in expanding their capacities to interact in a **We**Way

- Creates connection between people

- Cooperates with and engenders collaborative experiences

- Motivates and reinforces others

- Facilitates productive dialogue

- Easily able to move from conflict to co-creation in resolving issues

- Uses brainstorming as a decision making strategy

- Gives credit to others for their contributions

- Creates calm and order by his/her presence

- Promotes the sharing of diverse perspectives on issues

- Understands his or her perspective as one among many

- Before making decisions, gathers input from others that will be affected

- Makes decisions with a rationale that includes consideration of input received and how the decision is in alignment with guiding documents or relationship agreements

- Expresses empathy for others

- Provides data or takes action needed to stay in alignment with shared agreements

- Easily able to adapt to changes in directions

- Exhibits a good sense of humor

- Shows patience with others

- Gives and receives feedback constructively

- Good listener

- Mentors, coaches, and teaches others

- Maintains appropriate focus

- Is politically astute

- Is a good administrator and organizer

- Easily able to define his or her effect on others

- Seeks feedback

- Willingly shares knowledge

- Teaches others and participates interactively

- Leads in mending difficult situations

- Open to new ideas

- Stays open to all options

- Evokes, engenders, and experiences trust with others

- Maintains visionary understanding and big picture planning

- Provides a relaxed and focused presence in group meetings

- Creates and stays involved as a team or relationship member

- Manages time well

- Exhibits vulnerability appropriately

- Shares feelings and thoughts about issues

- Cooperates in relationships

The presence of any of these behaviors in a relationship has a positive effect on the capacity of the relationship or organization to fulfill its purpose. These behaviors can only be lived out because they are supported by interaction agreements. I can do my best to live out the *Black Ink Behaviors* listed above, yet I cannot consistently exhibit these **We**Way behaviors unless my partner or co-workers interact with me in ways that support them.

WeWay relational skills are the same skills commonly taught in a typical communication skills class. Active listening, reflection, dialogue, and brainstorming are all **We**Way communication skills; prevalent *Me*Way interaction patterns at home or in work relationships do not provide an environment supportive of such skills. Actually people who use **We**Way communication skills have often been shunned or demeaned when they suggest more collaborative means of making decisions.

In order to experience the positive behaviors of the **We**Way, the relational or organizational culture must support people in interacting in a **We**Way pattern of relating. Thus it is important that people take adequate time to create interaction agreements that reflect the shared genius of people in relationships and organizations. Until we all agree to interact differently - to change our pattern of relational interactions - it is likely that the negative *Red Ink Behaviors* will still appear in all relationships worldwide.

WeWay relationships and organizations don't spend much time managing conflict, because everyday differences of opinion are called forth, considered, and valued as important information that needs to be reviewed prior to making decisions. Diagram 3.2 shows the cooperative interaction pattern of how **We**Way organizations deal with conflict.

WeWay relationships and organizations provide places and times for different perspectives to be shared, valued, and validated. In fact, different opinions and perspectives on issues of importance are requested on a regular basis. Because everyone's input is valued, everyone feels confident that no matter what the issue, a positive solution will be co-created for everyone involved.

> *There is no perpetrator/victim or somebody/nobody paradigm in WeWay relationships and organizations. Diagram 3.2 shows that the blame game is not present and finding fault with others isn't tolerated.*

Mistakes are understood to be learning opportunities to grow deeper in understanding of one's work and relationships. **We**Way organizations are likely to offer some kind of reward for the biggest and best mistake made each year.

A good example of leadership the **We**Way is that of the crew on the starship *Enterprise* in the *Next Generation Star Trek* TV series. Like the *Enterprise* leadership team, members of **We**Way relationships and organizations understand that every day they are charting courses to go where no one has gone before. The past is the past and the future will be created based on where we choose to put our energy and attention. The past in **We**Way relational and organizational cultures is only good in terms of what can be learned from it. There is no time for debate about who was right or wrong, just the acknowledgment that something didn't work or isn't working any longer. A whole new idea is what will need to be created to solve situations where past strategies no longer work.

We can't solve today's problems using the same understanding that created them. Only a novel understanding that we manifest together can resolve the problems of this day and time. In all likelihood, the solution will be an amalgamation of a whole slew of individual ideas that meld together in a co-creative process, forging the path to be followed in the future.

WeWay people grow to be very comfortable with not knowing everything. They make it their purpose to gather information to make the best decisions that support everyone involved in the relationship to live in alignment with shared values and principles. **We**Way people know they are not alone in this life and that there are many talented and gifted people who, if asked, will help co-create a future that works for all. Because this is how people interact when issues or challenges arise, everyone feels safe and free to share their unique perspectives. Everything is on the table - nothing is withheld.

Jack spends time with Jill to determine whether or not the new job offer will enable them to live in alignment with their shared values. Jane spends time creating shared agreements that work for the whole team. Reverend Peter explores with the members of the congregation how to create a church where love is lived out in all relationships.

The bottom loop of Diagram 3.2 shows that because of the co-creative nature of dealing with issues and challenges, people assume everyone acts with best intentions toward others. It is assumed that people are doing the best they can, and improvement can only be accomplished with other people's support, additional education, and more information.

When we know that no matter what happens, our partners and co-workers will stand with us and grow with us while creating solutions that work for the common good, trust is engendered. When people realize that no matter the circumstances or conditions, we are truly in this together, they respond by being cooperative in their behavior. **We**Way people understand that they never have and never will accomplish anything alone. They know that dreams are only accomplished by taking individual and collective responsibility to stick together until a workable solution is created.

Just as with the *Me*Way pattern of behavior, it takes at least two or more human beings interacting to create a **We**Way pattern of behavior. Though one positive person can influence and motivate others to create a new pattern of interaction, the pattern itself requires the conscious and intentional participation of at least two or more people for it to become the foundation of interactions in the relationship or organization. Thus the importance of *understanding the difference* between *Me*Way and **We**Way relationships and organizations and *making the conscious choice to shift* from the *Me*Way to **We**Way interaction patterns.

> ***The value contained in co-creating written agreements cannot be overemphasized.***

Chapter 4: Making the Shift

To make a shift means literally choosing new dance steps in our relationships with other people, and having at least one other person do the new dance steps with us. There is no magic pill or formula that will make the shift happen; we learn the new dance by dancing and it requires a partner. Everyone's experience of making the shift is unique to them and the people they are relating with. There is no one way playbook, no definitive path that works for everyone all the time. Making the shift is a co-creative adventure and it takes at least two to Tango!

Here are the basic steps:

1. **Find a spouse, friend, or co-worker who is willing to commit to co-creating a WeWay relationship with you.** Simply put, **We**Way relationship building requires at least two or more people who create a conscious and intentional agreement. One person in any form of relationship can certainly live more in alignment with **We**Way behavior, and in doing so, other people in the relationship may change somewhat positively in response. However, when one person makes changes without the agreement of co-workers or co-members and tries to impose **We**Way expectations on the relationship partner, this most often creates resentment

and disconnection. Resentment and disconnection experienced in relationships are what create distrust and cause people to act without consideration of others. This is true even if the changes come from a place of best intentions and a desire to do no harm.

People in the *Me*Way commit acts of relational violence when they do things to other people without their agreeing to the action taken. Each time an act of violence is committed, another cycle of the *Me*Way interaction pattern present in command, control, and blaming relationships and organizations is triggered.

WeWay work is intended to be chosen freely by all participants so that a culture of collaboration, co-creation, and cooperative relationships can become a reality. It is impossible to coerce people to collaborate, co-create, and cooperate. When all relationship or organization members are part of the shift from a *Me*Way to a **We**Way pattern of interacting, they are much more willing to be held accountable to the new relationship.

2. **Invest in an educational and experiential learning experience to generate a shared under-standing of what living and working in a WeWay means for you and your partner(s), member(s), or co-worker(s).** This can be done by reading this book together and then using the samples in Appendixes A, B, and C to create your own ***Relational Interaction Agreement***. You may also choose to get this educational or experiential learning by taking a workshop together facilitated by a certified ***Relation-Shift Coach***. You can also choose to enter into a coaching relationship with a ***Relation-Shift Coach***, who can facilitate the educational and experiential learning experience uniquely for you and your relationship or organizational partners.

Couples can take this step in a weekend intensive while the average organization usually takes a week-long or two-weekend intensive.

3. **Co-create guiding documents that reflect your shared understandings.** People in committed personal relationships (married or other) create a relational inter-action agreement with an addendum that defines the partners' agreements regarding issues pertaining to the *8 Spheres of Relational Wholeness* (see Appendix A, Addendum A). If partners don't feel comfortable forming their initial agreement by themselves, it can also be facilitated by a *Relation-Shift Coach*. Follow-up coaching is available to help partners live into their agreement. A small work group (two to ten people) can go through the same experience.

For organizations consisting of multiple staff members and departments, it is best to invest in an assessment of the entire organization to define the desired culture and to co-create the guiding documents of the organization. If an organization or people in a relationship have acted in ways that have been strongly *Me*Way in the past, the non-decision makers usually don't trust the leaders or the dominant partner to conduct an assessment that reflects the true ideas of all people. Having an assessment performed by some-one outside the relationship or organization is a critical action that helps employees, spouses, and members know that this isn't just one more top-down attempt to persuade or cajole them into doing things the leader's way.

Once the assessment is completed, a *Relation-Shift Coach* can facilitate the formulation of guiding documents, provide coaching for leaders of organizations or relationship partners, and provide learning experiences crucial for shifting from the *Me*Way to the

WeWay. Once the initial assessment and education processes have been completed by a coach or **We**Way consultant and a collective decision has been made to change to **We**Way contexts, processes, and content, future assessments and education can be conducted by members of the relationship or the organization.

As a rule of thumb, the more relational anxiety, distrust, and independent action present in the current behaviors of organizational or relationship members, the more important it is to make the significant financial investment to have the assessment and educational offerings facilitated by a *Relation-Shift Coach*. Outside facilitation is often the only way to override the distrust present in *Me*Way organizations and to give people the best chance to co-create a **We**Way organization. It is fair to say that because people in *Me*Way organizations or relationships have often been so used to the common "us versus them" default pattern of interaction in cultures of command, control, and blaming relationships, they often need someone well-versed in the **We**Way to give them ideas of how to model **We**Way behavior in their relationships.

4. **Invest in working with a Relation-Shift Coach.** Living in a **We**Way is deeply attractive to most people, yet many people only know how to interact in a *Me*Way. Having a Relation-Shift Coach present (on staff internally or as an external presence) to mentor and educate relationship partners and/or organization employees or members serves to reinforce **We**Way behavior. Every person has his or her own learning curve in terms of becoming proficient in **We**Way behavior; therefore, providing adequate support to make the shift in behavior is essential.

Making the shift from *Me*Way to **We**Way relating is like learning a new language. When a person has only known and interacted from a *Me*Way perspective, it is initially challenging to remember to respond from a **We**Way perspective. People who make this shift most successfully have someone they can regularly check in with to reinforce the new language and behaviors. Investing in a Relation-Shift Coach helps people stay on track and keeps them in the habit of using the language and behaviors needed to ensure that **We**Way patterns of interaction occur on a consistent basis.

5. **Embed WeWay patterns of behavior in every aspect of the relationship and/or organization.** There is no such thing as doing some things in the *Me*Way and others in the **We**Way, although almost everyone attempts to do so initially in their learning process. Eventually, every situation, every issue, and every relationship has to come into alignment with the **We**Way of being for **We**Way relationships to become a reality. The exciting thing is that once a relationship or organization has experienced doing things the **We**Way, it is virtually impossible to return to doing things the *Me*Way without grave consequences (increased chaos, relationship drama, etc.).

A high level of chaotic, relational drama (distrust, gossip, politics), and conflict/crisis management occurs as a matter of course in MeWay relationships and organizations all the time. However, after even a short experience with the **We**Way, a return to doing things the *Me*Way increases people's awareness of the reality of the chaos, relational drama, and conflict/crisis management they have endured in the past. Those people new to the **We**Way often have the initial feeling that there is too much silence and that something is missing – and they are right!

Negative drama, stress and relational angst reduces dramatically as a WeWay relationship or organization emerges.

This is true, because people are no longer experiencing the high levels of relational anxiety that used to consume them in living the *Me*Way. Relational harmony, peace, and increased moments of silence are usual experiences in **We**Way organizations and relationships, and some people may initially interpret them as meaning something wrong is happening.

As people continue to embed the **We**Way of doing things in every aspect of their lives, the peace of relational harmony becomes a daily experience. It takes the average couple one to two years to leave most *Me*Way interacting patterns behind. It takes the average nonprofit organization or spiritual community at least five years to consistently live the **We**Way. It takes a business at least three years to embed the **We**Way into every department. The result of embedding the **We**Way in any relationship or organization is an increase in morale, relational harmony, trust, and productivity.

6. **Conduct at least an annual review of the WeWay *Relational Interaction Agreement*.** Reviewing guiding documents and relational agreements ensures that people are supporting them in living their shared principles and values in their interactions. A relational agreement gets fine-tuned over time as people gain practical experience living by it every day. In abiding by the agreement, people discover by experience what really works - or not - in helping them to live in alignment with their principles and values.

For instance, one work group learned the value of not engaging in faultfinding and blaming as a practice to keep them from reverting to their old *Me*Way behaviors. At the same time, they wanted to express their frustrations and concerns so that any information gleaned from their sharing, whether negative or positive, might help the group make better decisions in the future. So they revised their agreement to allow for a three-minute venting by any group member about an issue without any comment by the others listening to the venting. The group felt that this kept them from having to hide any true feelings and allowed them to be totally transparent when sharing all information. This way they could stay current and connected in relationship with others and do so without finding fault with them.

Relational agreements change as the people involved in the relationship or organization grow and mature in their understanding of living in a **We**Way. Since the **We**Way involves how we relate to others, the relational agreement becomes an evolving document that enables people to live in alignment with their principles and values. What works today to live in integrity with our principles and values may not work tomorrow. Regular reviews of shared agreements are crucial to sustaining relational and organizational integrity.

7. **Regularly seek out and build alliances with other people in WeWay relationships, work places, spiritual communities, and other forms of human organization.** People who are truly dedicated to creating a **We**Way world will find it more and more difficult to spend a lot of time with people who are content to interact from a *Me*Way perspective. It is also true that without a support system, **We**Way people are likely to see themselves reverting to *Me*Way behavior. The good news is that many forms of **We**Way relationships and organizations are continually being created. The next chapter reveals some of the ways the **We**Way is currently expressing in our world.

Chapter 5: Suggested WeWay Resources

It is good to know that we are never alone. The *Me*Way and the **We**Way exist in various forms throughout our world. The resources listed below provide compelling evidence of the dying of the *Me*Way and the need for the rising of the **We**Way worldwide.

> *Please note that no author of the resources below agreed that his or her work was in alignment with the material discussed in this book.*

By no means is this list exhaustive and readers are invited to submit other references to books, publications, spiritual communities, businesses, and other organizations that they believe are in alignment with the relational interaction pattern of the **We**Way described in this book. Readers are invited to help build a broader **We**Way community by participating in submitting other **We**Way references or resources at www.theweway.com.

1. Anderson, Carolyn and Roske, Katherine (2008). *The Co-Creator's Handbook: An Experiential Guide for Discovering Your Life's Purpose and Building a Co-Creative Society.* Global Family. Nevada City, California.

2. Barasch, Marc Ian (2005). *Field Notes on the Compassionate Life: A Search for the Soul of Kindness.* Rodale. Emmaus, Pennsylvania.

3. Beck, Donald and Cowan, Christopher (1996). *Spiral Dynamics.* Blackwell Publishing. Oxford, United Kingdom.

4. Berry, Thomas (1999). *The Great Work: Our Way Into the Future.* Three Rivers Press. New York, New York.

5. Buck, John and Villines, Sharon (2007). *We The People: Consenting to a Deeper Democracy, A Guide to Sociocratic Principles and Methods.* Sociocracy.info. Washington, D.C.

6. Bohm, David (1996). *On Dialogue.* Routledge. New York, New York.

7. Brown, Juanita; Isaacs, David and the World Café Community (2005*). The World Café: Shaping Our Futures Through Conversations That Matter.* Berrett-Koehler Publishers, Inc. San Francisco, California.

8. Campbell, Susan (1984). *Beyond the Power Struggle: Dealing with Conflict in Love and Work.* Impact Publishers. San Luis Obispo, California.

9. Campbell, Susan (2001). *Getting Real: 10 Truth Skills You Need to Live An Authentic Life.* H.J. Kramer and New World Library. Tiburon and Novato, California.

10. Childre, Doc and Martin, Howard (1999). *The HeartMath Solution: The Institute of HeartMath's Revolutionary*

Program for Engaging the Power of the Heart's Intelligence. HarperCollins Publishers. New York, New York.

11. Chopra, Deepak (2005). *Peace Is The Way: Bringing War and Violence To An End.* Harmony Books. New York, New York.

12. Dawlabani, Said Elias (2013). *MEMEnomics: The Next-Generation Economic System.* Select Books, Inc. New York, New York.

13. De Quincey, Christian (2002). *Radical Nature.* Invisible Cities Press. Montpelier, Vermont.

14. De Quincey, Christian (2005). *Radical Knowing.* Park Street Press. Rochester, Vermont.

15. Eisler, Diane and Loye, David (1990). *The Partnership Way: New Tools for Living and Learning, Healing Our Families, Our Communities and Our World.* Harper. San Francisco, California.

16. Flick, Deborah L. (1998). *From Debate to Dialogue: Using the Understanding Process to Transform Our Conversations.* Orchid Publications. Boulder, Colorado.

17. Frazee, Randy (2001*). The Connecting Church: Beyond Small Groups to Authentic Community.* Zondervan. Grand Rapids, Michigan.

18. Fuller, Robert (2003). *Somebodies and Nobodies*: *Overcoming the Abuses of Rank.* New Society Publishers. Gabriola Island, B.C., Canada.

19. Glaser, Judith E. (2005). *Creating We: Changing I-Thinking to WE-Thinking*. Platinum Press. Avon, Massachusetts.

20. Goleman, Daniel (2003). *Destructive Emotions: How Can We Overcome Them?* Bantam Books. New York, New York.

21. Graham, Lawrence Otis (1997). *Proversity: Getting Past Face Value and Finding The Soul of People*. John Wiley and Sons Inc. New York, New York.

22. Hacker, Stephen and Roberts, Tammy (2004). *Transformational Leadership: Creating Organizations of Meaning*. ASQ Quality Press. Milwaukee, Wisconsin.

23. Hawkins, David R. (1995). *Power vs. Force: The Hidden Determinants of Human Behavior*. Hay House Inc. Carlsbad, California.

24. Heifetz, Ronald A. (1994). *Leadership Without Easy Answers*. Belknap Press. Cambridge, Massachusetts.

25. Hollands, Jean A. (1997). *Red Ink Behaviors: Measure the Surprisingly High Cost of Problem Behaviors in Valuable Employees*. Blake/Madsen. Mountain View, California.

26. Holmes, Ernest (1926). *The Science of Mind*. G.P. Putnam's Sons. New York, New York.

27. Hubbard, Barbara Marx (1998). *Conscious Evolution: Awakening the Power of Our Social Potential*. New World Library. Novato, California.

28. Hubbard, Barbara Marx (2001). *Emergence: The Shift from Ego to Essence.* Hampton Road Publishing Company. Charlottesville, Virginia.

29. Jay, Mike R., et al. (2012). *@F-L-O-W: Find, Design, Use, Talent to Emerge Happiness and Success in a Postmodern World.* Leadership University Press. USA.

30. Johnson, Deborah, Rev. (2002). *Letters from the Infinite Volume One: The Sacred Yes.* New Brighton Books. Aptos, California.

31. Jones, W. Paul (2000). *Worlds Within A Congregation: Dealing with Theological Diversity.* Abingdon Press. Nashville, Tennessee.

32. Judith, Anodea (2006). *Waking the Global Heart: Humanity's Rite of Passage from the Love of Power to the Power of Love.* Elite Books. Santa Rosa, California.

33. King, Martin Luther (1967). *Where Do We Go from Here: Chaos or Community?* Harper & Row. New York, New York.

34. Korten, David C. (2006). *The Great Turning: From Empire to Earth Community.* Berrett-Koehler Publishers Inc. San Francisco, California.

35. Landau, Sy, Landau, Barbara and Landau, Daryl (2001). *From Conflict to Creativity.* Jossey-Bass. San Francisco, California.

36. Lewis, Thomas; Amini, Fari and Lannon, Richard (2000). *A General Theory of Love.* Vintage Books. New York, New York.

37. Loden, Marilyn (1996). *Implementing Diversity*. McGraw-Hill. New York, New York.

38. Mackey, John and Sisodia, Rajendra (2013). *Conscious Capitalism: Liberating the Heroic Spirit of Business*. Harvard Business Review Press. Boston, Massachusetts.

39. McIntosh, Steve (2012). *Evolution's Purpose: An Integral Interpretation of the Scientific Story of Our Origins*. Select Books Inc. New York, New York.

40. McLaughlin, Corinne and Davidson, Gordon (2010). *The Practical Visionary: A New World Guide to Spiritual Growth and Social Change*. Unity House. Unity Village, Missouri.

41. McTaggart, Lynne (2011). *The Bond: Connecting Through the Space Between Us*. Free Press. New York, New York.

42. Montuori, Alfonso and Conti, Isabella (1993). *From Power to Partnership: Creating the Future of Love, Work and Community*. Harper. San Francisco, California.

43. Quinn, Robert (1996). *Deep Change: Discovery of the Leader Within*. Jossey-Bass Publishers. San Francisco, California.

44. Quinn, Robert (2004). *Building the Bridge As You Walk On It: A Guide for Leading Change*. Jossey-Bass. San Francisco, California.

45. Ray, Paul and Anderson, Sherry Ruth (2000). *Cultural Creative: How 50 Million People Are Changing the World*. Three Rivers Press. New York, New York.

46. Rendle, Gilbert R. (1999). *Behavioral Covenants in Congregations: A Handbook for Honoring Differences.* The Alban Institute. Herndon, Virginia.

47. Rendle, Gilbert R. and Mann, Alice (2003). *Holy Conversations: Strategic Planning as a Spiritual Practice for Congregations.* The Alban Institute. Herndon, Virginia.

48. Risler, Diane (1987). *The Chalice and the Blade.* Harper & Row. San Francisco, California.

49. Robinson, Anthony B. (2003). *Transforming Congregational Culture.* William B. Eerdmans Publishing Company. Grand Rapids, Michigan.

50. Russell, Peter (1995). *The Global Brain Awakens: Our Next Evolutionary Leap.* Global Brain Inc. Palo Alto, California.

51. Sahtouris, Elisabet (2000). *EarthDance: Living Systems in Evolution.* iUniversity Press. Lincoln, Nebraska.

52. Sanders, Tim (2002). *Love Is the Killer App.* Three Rivers Press. New York, New York.

53. Scharmer, Otto and Kaufer, Katrin (2013). *Leading From the Emerging Future: From Ego-System to Eco-System Economics.* Berrett-Koehler Publishers, Inc. San Francisco, California.

54. Scharmer, C. Otto (2007). *Theory U: Leading from the Future as it Emerges – The Social Technology of Presencing.* Society for Organizational Learning. Cambridge, Massachusetts.

55. Scott, Susan (2002). *Fierce Conversations: Achieving Success at Work and In Life, One Conversation at a Time*. Viking Penguin. New York, New York.

56. Sellon, Mary K. and Smith, David (2005). *Practicing Right Relationship: Skills for Deepening Purpose, Finding Fulfillment and Increasing the Effectiveness in Your Congregation*. The Alban Institute. Herndon, Virginia.

57. Senge, Peter (1990). *The Fifth Discipline: The Art and Practice of the Learning Organization*. Currency Doubleday. New York, New York.

58. Senge, Scharmer; Jaworski, Joseph and Flowers, Betty Sue (2004). *Presence: Human Purpose and the Field of the Future*. The Society for Organizational Learning Inc. Cambridge, Massachusetts.

59. Spong, John (1998). *Why Christianity Must Change or Die*. Harper. San Francisco, California.

60. Spong, John (2001). *A New Christianity for a New World: Why Traditional Faith is Dying and How A New Faith is Being Born*. Harper. San Francisco, California.

61. Surowiecki, James (2004). *The Wisdom of Crowds: Why the Many Are Smarter Than the Few and How Collective Wisdom Shapes Business, Economies, Societies and Nations*. Doubleday. New York, New York.

62. Teilhard, de Chardin Pier (1959). *The Phenomenon of Man*. Harper & Brothers Publishers. New York, New York.

63. Tisch, Jonathan M. (2004). *The Power of We*. John Wiley & Sons Inc. Hoboken, New Jersey.

64. Twist, Lynne (2003). *The Soul of Money: Transforming Your Relationship with Money and Life*. W.W. Norton & Company. New York, New York.

65. Vistar Foundation: Founded by evolutionary pioneers, Dr. Ron Friedman and Victoria Friedman, Dedicated to Collective Evolutionary Consciousness for Collective Awakening, Co-creation and Conscious Communication; Featuring the *Vistar Method for Circles,* a Unified Field technology for groups, meetings, circles and gatherings. For more information: www.vistarfoundation.org.

66. Walsch, Neale Donald (2002). *The New Revelations*. Atria Books. New York, New York.

67. Wheatley, Margaret (2002). *Turning to One Another: Simple Conversations to Restore Hope to the Future*. Berrett-Koehler Publishers Inc. San Francisco, California.

68. Wheatley, Margaret (2005). *Finding Our Way: Leadership for an Uncertain Time*. Berrett-Koehler Publishers Inc. San Francisco, California.

69. Wilber, Ken (1996). *A Brief History of Everything*. Shambala Publications Inc. Boston, Massachusetts.

70. Wilkinson, Richard and Pickett, Kate (2009). *The Spirit Level: Why Greater Equality Makes Societies Stronger*. Bloomsbury Press. New York, New York.

71. Williams, Lloyd C. (1994). *Organizational Violence: Creating a Prescription for Change.* Quorum Books. Westport, Connecticut.

72. Williams, Lloyd C. (2002). *Creating the Congruent Workplace.* Quorum Books. Westport, Connecticut.

73. Wink, Walter (1992). *Engaging the Powers: Discernment and Resistance in a World of Domination.* Fortress Press. Minneapolis, Minnesota.

74. Wink, Walter (1998). *The Powers That Be: A Theology for a New Millennium.* Doubleday. New York, New York.

75. Woodhouse, Jack B. (1996). *Paradigm Wars: Worldviews for a New Age.* Frog Ltd. Berkeley, California.

Chapter 6: Common Objections to the WeWay

Many people throughout the world resonate with the need to shift from a *Me*Way to **We**Ways of being. At the same time, people who take action to make the shift experience discomfort because the **We**Way requires a willingness to do things in new ways. Even though you may love a new pair of shoes you recently purchased, you will probably experience some discomfort the first few times you wear them. Naturally you want to put on your old shoes to ease the pain, even though you'll eventually have to go back to the new ones. Here are the *few*, yet very common, discomforts you may experience when you commit to living life the **We**Way.

1. It takes time to work the WeWay.

Time is the biggest complaint that people have about being in and working in relationships with others from a **We**Way perspective. It is true that when two or more people agree to make the shift to a **We**Way of being in relationship or organization, they must learn how to do things differently. It takes the commitment of time and money to learn **We**Way conversation and decision making skills and to gather the input to co-create shared agreements. On the other hand, once the shared agreements have been created, people have a lot more freedom to move and act than they did in the *Me*Way. This freedom to act and move is possible because of the clear expectations and understandings present in the **Relational Interaction Agreement** and other guiding documents.

For instance, a district of franchise businesses was about to split in two due to a senior leadership issue. A Relation-Shift Coach was hired to help the businesses create guiding documents that expressed their shared agreements. These guiding documents clarified decision making criteria so that every franchise could manage their local business in alignment with district guiding documents. Prior to creating these documents, the district meetings took twelve hours a day for three days with little decision making occurring. After the documents were created, decision making for the group of businesses took less than an hour of time during one three-day session. It is amazing what a time saver these shared agreements are!

Operating the **We**Way means it actually takes less time to make decisions. People have a greater sense of autonomy in making day-to-day decisions in the organization once they are in agreement about decision making criteria. With guiding documents and **Relational Interaction Agreements** in hand, doing business the **We**Way takes a lot less time than doing things the *Me*Way.

The beauty in the long run of making the shift to the **We**Way is that people are able to make decisions faster due to their agreements about the criteria upon which decisions will be based. This levels the playing field for everyone. The same criteria for decision making are used for everyone from the CEO to the front-line mechanic on the assembly line. Everyone is then free to do his or her job with each person responsible to live in alignment with the shared criteria. As a result, decision making is expedited and people are able to spend the majority of their time delivering the service or product of the business.

Conversely, it is a myth that interacting in the *Me*Way takes less time. On the front end, the making of a unilateral decision and then issuing the order for the work to be done takes little time. It is the responses that others make once the unilateral decision is delivered that eats up people's time and energy, as well as financial, material, morale, mental, and emotional resources that will be expended because of the increase in the need for ongoing conflict management strategies.

A good example of this was the decision George W. Bush and Congress made to go to war in Iraq even though a large percentage of Americans and many of the most prominent countries in the world disagreed with the idea of war. Bush was not able to consider the issues in a **We**Way by taking the time needed to negotiate and collaborate. Instead he held his resolve to pre-emptively go to war with Iraq. As a result, though all our soldiers are now back from Iraq, years later America still has a significant image problem and a huge war-created debt load. Iraq will be in recovery for some time to come and with continued distain for all things American. On a global scale, we see that unilateral decisions will always carry with them a significant cost in debt and loss of human life, always increasing animosity between the unilateral decision-makers and those on whom the decisions are imposed.

Another example is the constant reorganization and reengineering actions that so many companies undergo. Instead of taking the time to create a shared agreement among the people in the company as to how the company will deal with reduced revenues, reconfiguring the customer base, changing markets and/or demands; most executives will cut jobs, limit the availability of financial resources, and announce a reorganization program. Yet every time there's a re-organization, the relationship matrix of people changes. People get new bosses and are moved into new department configurations. In the end little changes in the company because people don't have the trust or the camaraderie that makes successful recovery possible.

A prominent international corporation announced that yet another reorganizing and downsizing is slated for later this year. A senior director of the company remarked, "I wonder what would happen if they would just let us do our work. I've been through four reorganizations in the last three years. I have a new boss on the average of every nine months. We never know if we really are going to have a job or not. I have to constantly re-sell my group's charter to a new boss. I just get one new boss understanding our value and then here's yet one more internal customer I have to spend more time on. Is it any wonder why we don't have time to be working with external customers?"

"With each reorganization, my team is given more work to do in even smaller amounts of time. The pressure to perform is immense. As a result, stressed people make decisions that aren't about doing the right thing but doing the thing that will ensure they have a job down the road. No one trusts anyone. Everyone acts independently - it's all about personal survival these days. I wonder what it would be like if we weren't always operating out of fear of losing our jobs? I really care about my team members and their families. We've worked so hard to create relationships through which we work to do great things here and we've accomplished a lot. It just seems like such a waste. All the training and learning we did to be able to work together and then I have to choose which resource to eliminate."

"And doesn't the word 'resource' chalk all this up? That is what we call people here. We call them resources and we dispose of our resources and their incredible intellectual and wisdom capital with so little thought. Over time, the personal insecurity takes its toll on the ability of people to be present and do their work. Because people are scrambling for jobs and always looking for the good job somewhere else, I never have people's full attention. I lost two team members who went and found new jobs because they were tired of dealing with knowing they could lose their job any day and they knew I had no say in when or if that would happen. The number of hours I spend reassuring people, selling the value of my department, and establishing new relationships is incredibly costly. Doesn't the CEO know how much these reorganizations really cost, relationally? Is it any wonder that our quarterly results are so dismal? When you treat people like this you can't help but suffer in return."

The moral of the *Me*Way stories shared above is that when we don't take the time to include people in our decision making, it takes more of our time, energy, money, and attention in the long run. It *does take time* to build **We**Way relationships with people and it is worth every minute spent.

2. I can't make any decisions on my own in a WeWay relationship/organization.

This idea is false. Leaders and spouses make lots of decisions on their own in **We**Way relational cultures. The only difference is the decision making process used and each person taking the responsibility to make decisions in alignment with the shared agreements of the relationship or the organization. At all times, leaders and spouses must be able to provide a rationale regarding how they made decisions in alignment with the shared agreements of the relationship or the organization. The **We**Way commitment is to the shared agreements of the relationship or the organization, not to the personal opinion, expert knowledge, or perspective of one person in a relationship or a few people in an organization.

In a business, one of the most critical shared agreements involves what happens when a project escalation occurs and a fast decision is needed. What if time is limited? It may be that the organization decides that someone be given the authority to make a quick decision. From a **We**Way perspective, the person given the decision making authority when speed is important gets that authority from the shared agreement of the group *before* project escalations occur. This individual then makes a decision in certain circumstances not because of his or her position title but because his or her decision will best enable the organization to live in integrity and accomplish its goals. When everyone knows the process in advance, things go much more smoothly and effectively because everyone is in agreement or "on the same page".

Shared agreements spell out the criteria that everyone understands will be used to say "yes" or "no" to certain propositions. Once the shared criteria in the form of written agreements exist, people can make all the necessary decisions without needing to get permission from others to do so. Thus, less time is spent in meetings and more time in increased enjoyment at home, and at work, every day.

3. I have to base my decisions on the collective wisdom of the group versus my own opinion.

Absolutely. This is the core skill of **We**Way relationships and organizations. To live in the **We**Way requires the understanding that there is no one person who has the right answer. In fact, if one is able to live the **We**Way, he or she *gives up being right as a goal in a relationship*. There is no right answer. There is a next best answer to every issue. However, that next best answer is one that can only be found by gathering the collective intelligence of all people in the relationship or the organization.

To live in the **We**Way requires learning how to value and celebrate all the different perspectives, information, and life experience people bring to a relationship or an organization. At the same time, one has to learn how to allow for or yield to the collective intelligence of the group as regards decision making, simply because all of us are actually smarter than any one of us, as documented in the book *The Wisdom of Crowds,* by James Surowiecki.

This doesn't refer to rule by majority vote. This refers to rule by collective intelligence of ideas that are gathered and on which a thematic analysis is performed. **We**Way decision making processes are collective discernment processes. Decisions are made based on whether they are or are not in alignment with the shared decision making criteria outlined in an organization or relationship's shared agreements. We say "yes" to decisions that we discern will keep us in alignment with our shared principles, values, and goals.

The opinion of any individual in **We**Way living and working is simply considered as a bit of information or knowledge to be aware of in a decision making process. In the **We**Way, personal opinions or bits of information or knowledge aren't debated, though all of these are deemed to be of equal value. Instead, solutions that work to maintain relational or organizational integrity are co-created. A creative process is used to discover solutions that everyone knows to the best of their ability, based on the facts of today, will enable them to "walk their talk". The **We**Way is ultimately about *our walking our talk* instead of you walking your talk and me walking my talk. We walk in the direction of our collective intelligence and wisdom, not individual expertise or opinion. We are smarter than me!

4. I cannot create a WeWay relationship by myself.

True. A **We**Way relationship is one that is lived consciously and intentionally by at least two people who do the following:

- Expend the effort and invest the time (and money) to co-create a ***Relational Interaction Agreement*** and any other needed documents that name the shared understandings of how life or work will be lived.

- Commit to living in alignment with those shared agreements in relationship to any issue that arises.

- Regularly review and (if need be) modify the agreements to ensure that they reflect what is true for the relationship or organization today.

People who are committed to living and working the **We**Way get better at it as time passes. It takes time to weed out *Me*Way behavior and ways of being. Additionally, it takes time to word agreements in a way that reflects what really works for people in a particular situation. Many people find that their initial agreements, though good in general, reflect what was good based on what their families of origin or society said about how one ought to engage in personal relationships or structure business relationships. Over time, **We**Way people modify their agreements to reflect their unique understanding of what enables them to know relational or organizational integrity.

Sometimes couples or organizations will initially choose to use one of the example agreements found in the appendixes of this book. This gives them time to see what works or doesn't work for them before they write an agreement that truly reflects their unique relationship or organization. We all have to start somewhere, so if one of the example agreements works for you, please use it. The good thing is that the example agreements are written to accurately reflect the **We**Way culture of collaboration, co-creation, and cooperative relationships. You can't go wrong using these examples as a way to learn more about living in the **We**Way.

A **We**Way relationship or organization means one in which at least two or more people have participated in co-creating shared agreements that they are living in alignment with every day. All expectations about the relationship or organization are freely shared and known to everyone else. There are no secrets. People don't hope they're on the same page as their relationship partner or co-worker; they know they are on the same page. There is no guessing about whether they are on the same team or not. *People are obligated to speak up should any new expectation arise so that it can be considered by others.*

A **We**Way team at work knows it is a team because all of its members have talked about their expectations, gleaned their collective wisdom, and have written an agreement that each team member abides by in their interactions with each other, every day. It is not an option to interact outside of the agreement or to withhold any newly revealed expectations. If the agreement needs to be modified then everyone takes the time to do this so that they stay on the same page with one another.

No one can do the **We**Way to anyone else. Two or more people have to choose and live the **We**Way together for it to be a successful venture. The **We**Way is done with other people. It is a co-created reality and impossible to do by oneself.

Chapter 7: A Personal Note

"The caged bird sings because it must. Sometimes the melody arrived at in the cage is much more fetching, much more appealing, much more profound, much more poignant than the melody arrived at by the bird who is on the loose. 'The caged bird sings with a fearful trill, its song is heard on the distant hill. For the caged bird sings of freedom.' *There is something universal about that song since all of us are caged in some way or another. So all of us can hear it and say, 'Oh Yes', let that bird out. Let it sing that song."*
-Maya Angelou as aired on "Soul Sunday" with Oprah Winfrey, September 8, 2013

My caged bird song of the **We**Way, was forged through the crucible of my own life experience of human relationship. If the **We**Way calls to you, I invite you to consider making the daring shift to do whatever it takes to leave the prison bars of the *Me*Way pattern of interaction behind in your personal and professional life. I am convinced that shutting the doors on the *Me*Way interaction pattern in human relationships is a core requirement for the future evolution of the human race.

It is time that you and I unlock the key to our collective heart to walk as "WE" into a more

glorious future. It is time that the love and respect that every human being deserves comes to be known consciously and intentionally in our daily interactions with one another.

I have learned that I can yearn for, pray for, and talk about; love, joy, peace, respect, harmony, intimacy and never know the experience of those deeply divine longings of the collective human soul in my daily interactions. I have only realized the experience of these universal spiritual qualities in relationships as I have dared through making agreements with others, to behave in ways that assure these qualities can be known in the flesh of our daily interactions. God, the *All that Is* called by many names, only acts in and through us and will never do for us what we are destined to do in partnership with one another.

If love and respect for one another is to be our shared future realtiy, it will be because you and I dared one day to make the conscious choice to forge and abide by new WeWay agreements in all relationships at home, at work, and especially in the halls of government worldwide.

We must finally learn that we can't shift or change what we aren't willing to talk about. We must be brave in identifying the *Me*Ways in our relationships as that which will never co-create the love and respect we say we desire. We must be equally as brave and courageous to co-create new, **We**Ways of interaction and commit to returning to them when we fall back into our *Me*Ways, as we will surely do.

My wife and I, tired of several failed *Me*Way relationship experiences, started our relationship differently. Instead of just hoping our relationship experience would be different, we invested our time, money and minds for three days with my business coach. In three days, he walked us through my model of **The WeWay Relational Development System** that I use in my coaching and consulting practice. We left that weekend with our **We**Way *Relational Interaction Agreement* that set the context for the harmonious life we now live out in our interactions everyday.

> *Relationships only fail because partners*
> *fail to meet 100% of the needs and expectations*
> *of those involved.*

Instead of the growing apart and fading intimacy we had experienced in previous relationships, we continue to grow closer and more deeply intimate in ways we never thought possible in our *Me*Way days. Our shared expectations of what our "WE" is guides and directs our daily interactions so that relational harmony is our everyday experience at home, work, and play. We know that our transparent sharing of our expectations through co-creating our agreement is the reason we know the depth of love, respect, and joy in our relationship.

We review our agreement at least every year and have made changes as we came to know each other better. As a result, our agreement has self-organized itself into our unique, authentic "WE" which has been made possible by our willingness to be totally transparent and committed to meeting 100% of the needs of each partner in the relationship.

Living life the **We**Way at home and at work does not keep the somebody-nobody game of the *Me*Way from knocking at our relationship's door nor from knocking at the door of the Center for Consciousness Education (a **We**Way-based organization, that I serve as Director). There have been a couple of very trying times in which we could have chosen to revert to *Me*Ways of interacting and been done with each other and/or closed the Center and given up.

Yet, as of this day, I am grateful to be able to say, we have dared to interact according to our agreements and an even more deeply authentic love and a deep respect for one another has emerged to grace our days.

Whoever the "WE" is that you or I might have concern about is a "WE" that is daily co-creating using the invisible, yet palpable, interaction patterning of MeWay or WeWay. If you or I don't like our "WE" experience, it will only change if we both, or we all, agree to interact differently.

I know down to the marrow of my bones that we innately have the capability to do this relational work as human beings. Evolution seeded this ability in the guts of each one of us and is now pulling our heart strings through the painful result of our *Me*Ways, encouraging us to choose anew this day.

The good news – there is a better way – the WeWay.

I offer the model and methodology of the **We**Way as depicted in this book, not as "the" perfect answer nor the answer for everyone. The **We**Way is one of many viable vehicles through which love, respect, kindness, and care for all life may bloom more consciously into all forms of relationship in our lives. In deed, in times of the prospect of severing relationship for good, the **We**Way has served to keep so many people at table and talking about co-creating different ways of being in relationship through which love, deeper respect and even greater prosperity eventually emerged.

The good news is that the **We**Way relational interaction pattern is rising up as a life-giving option and being addressed in may ways. As a result, a renewed sense of hope that the continued evolution of the human race and that of our Earth can indeed be a magnificent one. It is simply a matter of choosing to change how we interact with one another. If you are ready to make a shift to interacting differently in your personal and professional relationships, know that you are not alone and that help into living life the **We**Way is a simple phone call or mouse click away.

Please **DO** use the *Relational Interaction Agreements* in this book as templates for forming your own agreements. For information about **We**Way coaching, teaching and facilitation services for forming *Relational Interaction Agreements* for couples, corporations, religious/spiritual communities, or work groups/teams, or to inquire about becoming a certified **We**Way Relation-Shift Trainer and Coach, please contact Wendy Foxworth online at www.theweway.com or via e-mail at www.wendyfoxworth@aol.com or call 505-514-2024.

Appendix A: Relational Interaction Agreement for Couples/Life Partners

To the end that we live in relational harmony all the time, it is our intent to commit our thinking, our speaking, and our acting so as to live in alignment with these relational interaction guidelines that take into consideration our shared understanding about the eight spheres of our relationship.

This agreement of relational interaction describes a pattern of interpersonal behavior that we, _____ and _____, agree to abide by regardless of situations that arise to be dealt with. It is with this agreement that we recognize that how we are in relationship with one another is and ever will be the most important issue of importance regardless of what we ever accomplish in terms of what we do or what form our relationship takes. We agree to do only things that support us to create and sustain loving relationships of goodwill between ourselves, our families, our friends, our local communities, and the world at large.

To this end, we commit to creating, implementing, and sustaining a relational culture of consideration, co-creation, and cooperative relationships. We agree to uphold the following core beliefs and behaviors in our relationships with one another and in our relationships with those who are served through our relationship:

A. HOW WE MAKE DECISIONS: Believing that the actions we take will always affect each other and other people, before making any decision to act on anything that affects any sphere of our relationship, each of us will gather together and take into account the input of those people who may be affected by any action that is being considered. Before any decision is made, we ask ourselves the following questions:

1. What decision will best allow us to stay in relational harmony?

2. Have I received the input of everyone who will be affected by this decision and adjusted my decision so it takes into account the collective wisdom?

All decisions will be made in alignment with this agreement. At all times, each person is held accountable to state how his/her decisions were made in alignment with this agreement to achieve shared goals.

B. HOW WE USE OUR RESOURCES: We use our combined resources (money, intellectual property, physical property, history, personal life experience, and network of personal and professional relationships) to support our shared agreements and to realize each person's full potential.

C. HOW WE STAY CURRENT ABOUT OUR THOUGHTS AND FEELINGS IN OUR RELATIONAL INTERACTIONS: We take the responsibility to proactively own and share our individual thoughts and feelings about any situation of mutual concern whether we consider our thoughts and feelings to be negative or positive. In this way, we stay above board in sharing what we are thinking and feeling so we can make the best possible decisions regarding any situation. We find time each week to check-in and confirm that we are clear and current with each other.

D. HOW WE AGREE TO BE IN RELATIONSHIP WITH OTHERS: We accept and embrace each partner's choice to create individual support outside of the relationship that honors and supports the relationship. We support strategies that enhance our wellness within all spheres of our relationship. We show our love, speak our truth, are authentic, care about people, are accountable and responsible in our music, work, play, and life with one another and we agree to challenge our friends, family, and co-workers to do the same.

E. HOW WE DEAL WITH CONFLICT: Believing with Gil Rendle that "conflict is the presence of two or more ideas in the same place at the same time," when conflict occurs, we will accept that no one's individual opinion is a sufficient solution for the issue at hand. When this occurs we will take the time necessary to listen to each person's ideas. We will honor and respect each other by not interrupting when ideas are shared. We will accept at face value and not debate the validity of any idea shared. We will view all ideas as valid information to be considered. Once all ideas have been shared we will work together to create a new collective solution that will work for the mutual benefit of both of us. We will seek outside guidance if we are unable to co-create a solution that works to keep us connected in oneness with God and each other. Above all we agree to stay in the room with each other and never go to bed angry or without having reached an agreement about what our next step will be to resolve a particular issue.

F. WHEN THINGS DO NOT GO AS PLANNED (OR AS WE WANT THEM TO): Believing that each of us is of esteemed value, we will assume that each person has good intentions as regards their involvement and actions in any situation. When things do not go the way we want them to or as we have planned, individually or collectively, and we find ourselves upset or in faultfinding or blaming behavior, we will stop and acknowledge that it is likely that we have slipped back into the culture of command, control, and blaming relationships. When this occurs we agree to stop our conversation, ask for forgiveness if necessary, acknowledge that a slip has occurred, and then shift back to dealing with the situation in alignment with this agreement.

We will treat any slip into old behavior as a learning opportunity or teaching moment in which we are given the additional practice time to experience co-creating and collaborating to build answers and solutions to life's challenges that work for both of us.

In particular, when either of us or both of us goes into a need to faultfind, to blame ourselves or others, we will stop and ask the person exhibiting the behaviors to look at their need for such behavior.

G. REASSESS OUR AGREEMENT ANNUALLY AND REVISE IF NECESSARY.

_____   _____

Linda Tool   Date   Sam Wade   Date

Addendum A

8 SPHERES OF RELATIONAL WHOLENESS

SPIRITUAL

- ❏ We have strong individual spiritual paths

- ❏ We do together activities that support our spiritual path

- ❏ We have a decision making process that is grounded in our spiritual principles

- ❏ We have shared practices that we do as a couple: we meditate, go to community once a week, and do workshops and pray together

- ❏ We pray and do a daily reading from a "Day at a Time"

- ❏ We attend the Revelation Conference at the Agape International Spiritual Center

SOCIAL/RELATIONAL

- ❏ We host small home-based group parties to do activities like playing cards and Wii

- ❏ We watch basketball and attend regional and final four games when possible

- ❏ We do for each other without having to be asked

- ❑ There is an ease with which we interact with each other

- ❑ We pay attention to balancing our social time with others, our together time, and our individual alone time

- ❑ We participate in creating and sustaining family relationships

- ❑ We include family and friends and uphold our relationship agreement when we are with them

- ❑ We participate in social events at our spiritual community

EMOTIONAL

- ❑ We have the ability to identify and verbally articulate our feelings

- ❑ We have the ability to listen to each other without taking it personally or having to fix the other person

- ❑ We have mutual maturity levels

- ❑ We own our own sides about our interactions because we know it takes two to tango – we are accountable/responsible for our own stuff

- ❑ We do not make decisions based on previous family or ex-partner experiences or our own addiction histories

INTELLECTUAL

- ❑ We have a mutual capability to engage, understand, and initiate conversations about philosophy, spirituality, and world affairs

- We have a mutual commitment to expand our knowledge base and to continually learn by continually reading books and attending seminars/workshops at least once a year

- We involve ourselves in learning more about relational development, change, acceptance, diversity, and globalization issues

PHYSICAL

- We will hire a personal trainer to design a getting in shape and/or core strengthening regime

- After getting in shape, Sam will do Saturday morning basketball or boxing

- Linda will do regular Pilates by herself or with an instructor

- We will ride the recumbent bike at least three times a week

- We get regular physical check-ups at least annually

- We eat in healthy ways

- Sam's Skinny eating plan

- Linda's use of Hawkins losing weight plan

- Linda to be in size 18 and Sam gets to size 34

- Reciprocity is present that assures both partners are nurtured physically and sexually

- ❑ Oneness is experienced that is not personality-based

- ❑ Lack of self-consciousness is present in our interactions; we have fun and laugh a lot

- ❑ We regularly have holding and talking time

- ❑ We have a clean, spacious, simple, and orderly home that exudes a feeling of peace and warmth to all who visit it

- ❑ Linda will assist Sam in irrigating the yard and pruning the bushes and trees

- ❑ Linda will do the gardening and yard care as part of her get-in-shape program

- ❑ We pick up after ourselves, not expecting the other to clean up after us

- ❑ We plan and take two vacations a year; one spiritual and one for fun

- ❑ Sam will tell Linda when it is time to pay bills and Linda will help

- ❑ Household repairs will be taken care of by the person who spends most time at home, and the traveling-to-work person will assist when appointments can be made at least one to two weeks in advance

- ❑ We will create a budget/financial investment/retirement/ spending plan that reflects alignment with our *Relational Interaction Agreement* by April 30, 2013

- Linda will put together a realistic budget proposal for this year based on spending last year

- Linda will open a new account and do regular balancing of her checkbook

- Sam reviews Linda's checkbook records monthly and collaborates in the decision about how much money will be paid to get the credit card debt paid off

- We develop a plan of action to care for each other should either person become disabled and not be able to contribute financially at all

- Finish our funeral plan book

- We make major financial decisions over $500 in consultation with each other

- Both of us contribute financially

- We receive and are continually open to receiving an abundance of material and financial resources so that peace, plenty, and relational wholeness can be experienced by others and ourselves

MORALS

- We are inclusive in our relationships with other people

- We appreciate differences and learn much from different people in our lives

- We are considerate of each other and our neighbors

- ❑ We are acceptant of a variety of family combinations or created extended families

- ❑ We know we are all one as a human race and our differences are a blessing

- ❑ We follow civic law, abide by it, and get involved to change laws that are unjust

- ❑ We are for human rights of all people

- ❑ We work toward creating a sustainable future for humanity and our planet

- ❑ We support each other in being true to who we are and supporting each other's perpetual growth and development

VALUES

- ❑ We value relational harmony

- ❑ We are world-centric

- ❑ We value personal and collective integrity

- ❑ We value supporting each other in fulfilling our individual callings

- ❑ We value the principles of oneness, trust, truth, kindness, and generosity

SELF-IDENTITY

- ❏ We know ourselves to be members of the human race and we are here to be of service to others and our planet

- ❏ We are each endowed with certain gifts and abilities that we use not only for individual good but also for the good of our relationship, and our relationships with other human beings

- ❏ We accept a caregiving role in our relationship with mother earth, and co-creating a sustainable future is the way we will maintain that connection

- ❏ We are in relationship to support each other in fulfilling our spiritual paths and to fulfill our soul callings to the end that we do our evolutionary best to increase the consciousness of the human race with every thought, word and deed

Appendix B: Relational Interaction Agreement for a Work Team/Group

This agreement of relational interaction describes a pattern of interpersonal behavior that we, **Members of the Business Assurance Team,** agree to abide by regardless of situations that arise to be dealt with. It is with this agreement that we recognize that how we are in relationship with one another is and ever will be the most important issue regardless of what we ever accomplish in terms of business contracts. It is through our relationships that our work is accomplished. Therefore, we take the time in this agreement to establish respectful and considerate working relationships. If needed, we agree to make specific amendments to this agreement as regards particular business situations.

Together we commit to creating, implementing, and sustaining a culture of collaboration, co-creation, and cooperative relationships as a team. We agree to uphold the following core beliefs and behaviors in our relationships with one another and with those who we interact with:

1. **HOW WE MAKE DECISIONS:** Believing that the actions we take will always affect other people, before making any major decision to act, we will note who will be affected and

involve him or her in the decision making process. When we do need to involve other team members, we agree to:

❑ Communicate (via phone and e-mail) to solicit the input of those people who may be affected by any action that is being considered; we agree to respond to any phone call or e-mail within a business day (taking into consideration time zones and travel schedules)

❑ All phones need to accept international calls

❑ First words in the e-mail subject line to help everyone to respond in a timely manner:

  o FYI

  o ACTION

  o URGENT

  o HELP

❑ To be accountable to one another, each person will state how his or her decisions were made in alignment with this agreement and any shared goals

2. SPECIFIC STRUCTURES FOR WEEKLY MEETINGS:

❑ The director's administrative assistant will act as the timekeeper for meetings

❑ Each team member will send items he or she needs to have discussed at the weekly meeting to the assistant no later than 12:00 noon Pacific time on Mondays. The assistant will send out a reminder for agenda items on Fridays. Each agenda item request needs to include the following:

  o Time needed

  o Whether this is INFORMATION or A DECISION IS NEEDED

  o Who should lead in addressing the item

  o Which week's agenda it needs to be on

❑ Etiquette: team members will be on the call or changes can be made about the call only if able to give 24-hour notice

❑ Let the team know if you will not be on the call with as much advance notice as possible. The assistant will include this information on the agenda

❑ The assistant will review agenda with the director before sending out to team members

❑ Calls will be Tuesdays at 11:00 a.m. Pacific time, USA

3. **HOW WE DEAL WITH EACH OTHER WHEN THINGS DON'T GO AS PLANNED:** Believing that every person has good intentions in regards to their involvement

and actions they take in any situation, when things do not go as we have planned:

- ❑ We will focus on the issue and not spend time faultfinding and blaming anyone

- ❑ We will work together to create a constructive solution by "dialoging" about the situation to clarify the issue. We will then brainstorm together to create and implement a solution that is of mutual benefit to all those involved

- ❑ We will ask for help when needed

4. **HOW WE STAY CURRENT ABOUT OUR THOUGHTS AND FEELINGS ABOUT OUR RELATIONAL INTERACTIONS:** We take the responsibility to:

- ❑ Be open and share our thoughts and concerns with each other

- ❑ Be always willing to share all the knowledge we have about a particular situation whether we judge it to be positive or negative

- ❑ Keep the team collaboration site up to date with current status of the initiative we own, so information is complete

- ❑ We will post attachments or other documents to the team collaboration site vs. sending an e-mail

- ❑ Log into Skype on a daily basis

5. **HOW WE RESPECT AN INDIVIDUAL'S NEED FOR WORK/LIFE BALANCE:** We embrace the attitude "working to live" rather than "living to work." Outside of core office hours, typically between 8:00 a.m. and 6:00 p.m. local time in any time zone, we may have differing commitments to family, partners, or other personal interests.

   ❑ We understand that people who attend conference calls outside their core hours may need to occasionally miss a call due to personal obligations

   ❑ If we are unable to attend a scheduled out-of-hours call we will give as much notice as possible to the administrative assistant and/or the call facilitator

   ❑ We will try, wherever possible, not to schedule very long days or very short days by scheduling two conference calls. This is acceptable only on an occasional basis for ad hoc calls and on a monthly basis at the very most for regular calls

   ❑ We will accept and encourage people on very early or very late calls to take time off during the day to help redress work/life balance

   ❑ We will watch how often we personally touch base, and use messaging to connect with those who feel isolated due to our worldwide roles

   ❑ We will go to a corporate building office when needed

   ❑ We will plan meetings face-to-face as much as we are able

6. **HOW WE DEAL WITH CONFLICT:** Believing that no one's individual opinion is a sufficient solution for any particular issue at hand; when conflict occurs:

- ❏ We will take the time necessary to listen to the ideas of everyone involved

- ❏ We will not interrupt people when they are sharing their ideas and we will not debate the validity of any idea shared to practice honoring the offerings of others

- ❏ We will speak up if we feel we are not being listened to

- ❏ We will view all ideas as valid information to be considered

- ❏ Once all ideas have been shared we will work together to create a new collective solution that will work for the mutual benefit of all people involved

- ❏ We will agree together to involve an independent party (another team member or the director) if we cannot create a solution within a certain timeframe

- ❏ We will not involve an independent party or escalate before we spend time dialoging with involved parties to see if a resolution can be found

7. **WHAT WE DO WHEN WE REGRESS TO BLAMING/ GUILT-TRIPPING OR COMMAND AND CONTROL, UNILATERAL DECISION MAKING BEHAVIOR:** Believing that we (at times) will slip back into behaving in these ways, we will:

❑ Stop our conversation and acknowledge that a 'slip' has occurred

❑ Ask for forgiveness in having made the slip

❑ If needed, an individual can vent frustration or anger about an issue for 1–2 minutes without comment from, or discussion by other team members

❑ After venting is complete, we will shift back to dealing with the situation in alignment with our culture of co-creation and collaborative relationships as outlined in this document

❑ We will treat any slip in our behavior as a learning opportunity or teaching moment in which we are given the additional practice time to experience co-creating mutually beneficial solutions and collaborative relationships

As a part of **the Business Assurance Team**, the signatures below signify each member's commitment to abide according to this agreement and to any future modifications made upon reviewing this document at least every three months:

_____   _____

(position title and name)   (date)

_____   _____

(position title and name)   (date)

Appendix C: Relational Interaction Agreement for a Corporation

This agreement of relational interaction describes a pattern of interpersonal behavior that we, members of the board of directors, the CEO, department managers, and employees of **the ABC Corporation**, agree to abide by regardless of situations that arise to be dealt with. We know that it is the quality of our interpersonal relationships that creates the vehicle for our being able to accomplish corporate and department goals.

Therefore, with our company values of teamwork, transparency, excellence, partnership, productivity, positivity, and respectful relationships, we have co-created this agreement that makes explicit how all members will behave interpersonally so that our values can be our lived reality.

It is with this agreement that we recognize that how we are in relationship with one another is and ever will be the issue of importance regardless of what we accomplish in terms of business productivity. Each department within the corporation will be responsible to ensure that all its actions and decisions are made in alignment with this agreement.

Together we commit to creating, implementing, and sustaining a culture of collaboration, co-creation, and cooperative relationships. We agree to uphold the following core beliefs and behaviors in our relationships with one another and in relationships with those we interact with in all business affairs:

1. **HOW WE MAKE DECISIONS:** Believing that the actions we take will always affect other people, before making any major decision to act, each member will:

   ❏ Make decisions using the 10 Step **We**Way Decision Making Process (see Appendix E).

   ❏ Trust that each individual knows when others need to be involved in the process.

   ❏ When we do need to involve other members we agree to communicate via phone or e-mail to solicit the input of those people who may be affected by any action that is being considered.

   ❏ We agree to hold each member accountable to state how his or her decisions were made in alignment with this agreement and any shared goals.

2. **HOW WE DEAL WITH EACH OTHER WHEN THINGS DON'T GO AS PLANNED:** Believing that every person has good intentions in their involvement and actions they take in any situation, when things do not go as planned, we will:

   ❏ Focus on the issue and not spend time faultfinding and blaming anyone.

❑ Work together to create a constructive solution by "dialoging" about the situation to clarify the issue. We will then brainstorm together to create and implement a solution that is of mutual benefit to all those involved.

❑ Ask for help when needed.

3. **HOW WE STAY CURRENT ABOUT OUR THOUGHTS AND FEELINGS ABOUT OUR RELATIONAL INTERACTIONS:** We take the responsibility to:

❑ Be open and share our thoughts and concerns with each other, whether positive or negative.

❑ Share all the knowledge we have about a particular situation. We also agree to keep the department collaboration sites up to date with current status of the initiative any member owns, so information is complete.

❑ Post attachments to the company collaboration site vs. sending an e-mail,

4. **HOW WE RESPECT AN INDIVIDUAL'S NEED FOR WORK/LIFE BALANCE:** We all embrace the attitude "working to live" rather than "living to work." Outside of core office hours, typically between 8:00 a.m. and 6:00 p.m. local time, we may have differing commitments to family, partners, or other personal interests. Therefore, we will:

❑ Understand that people who attend conference calls outside their core hours may need to occasionally miss a call due to personal obligations

- ❑ Call the facilitator/lead of a conference call if we are unable to attend a scheduled out-of-hours call, taking care to give as much notice as possible

- ❑ Accept and encourage people on very early or very late calls to take time off during the day to help redress work/life balance

- ❑ Watch how often we personally touch base, and use messaging to help ease the isolation felt due to our worldwide roles

- ❑ Go to the corporation office as often as needed

- ❑ Plan face-to-face meetings at least two times a year for all departments

5. **HOW WE DEAL WITH CONFLICT:** Believing that no one's individual opinion is a sufficient solution for any particular issue at hand, when conflict occurs we will:

- ❑ Take the time necessary to listen to the ideas of everyone involved

- ❑ Not interrupt others when they are sharing their ideas and not debate the validity of any idea shared in order to practice accepting one another at face value

- ❑ Speak up if we feel we are not being listened to

- ❑ View all ideas as valid information to be considered.

❑ Work together to create a new collective solution that will work for the mutual benefit of all people involved.

❑ Not involve an independent party or escalate before we spend time dialoging to see if a resolution can be found.

❑ Agree together to involve an independent party if we cannot create a solution within a certain timeframe.

6. **WHAT WE DO WHEN WE REGRESS TO OLD COMMAND, CONTROL, AND BLAMING RELATIONSHIP BEHAVIOR**: Believing that we at times will slip back into behaving in old ways, we will:

❑ Stop our conversation and acknowledge that a 'slip' has occurred

❑ Ask for forgiveness if necessary or ask for 1–2 minutes of vent time

❑ Shift back to dealing with the situation in alignment with our culture of collaboration, co-creation, and cooperative relationships as outlined in this document

❑ Treat any slip into blaming relationship behavior as a learning opportunity or teaching moment in which we are given the additional practice time to experience co-creating mutually beneficial solutions and collaborative relationships

My signature signifies my commitment to abide by the tenets of this agreement and to any future modifications made in the review of this document by the ABC Corporation each year:

_____ _____

(Lead Engineer, Mark Allen)　　　(date)

_____ _____

(Human Resource
Department Manager
Sally Smith)　　　(date)

Appendix D: Relational Interaction Agreement for a Religious/ Spiritual Community

Definition of the Relational Interaction Agreement for the Center for Consciousness Education (CCE)

Our **Relational Interaction Agreement** describes an interpersonal pattern of behavior. All staff, leaders, and team members agree to abide by this agreement. Therefore, newcomers and people of the broader community see in action how we live in alignment with our purpose, principles, practices, and plans for CCE programming. This agreement reflects the collective wisdom of CCE participants.

This agreement serves as the basis of how we sustain organizational and relational integrity. This is our talk *and* our walk. Our intent is that all paid staff members, CCE leaders, and team members (volunteers) will interact in ways that embody the spiritual quality of love. This is how we choose to interact with one another.

This is the primary guiding document of our center. It behaviorally states how we agree to embody integrity in our interactions.

It is with this agreement that we recognize how we are in relationship with one another is the most important aspect of our spiritual community regardless of what we accomplish in organizational goals or programs.

We understand that the goals and programs we create are forms that will change over time. That which is eternal is our spiritual purpose, principles, and practices. Growth in number, funding, or in physical assets is only important if the work to acquire them supports us in living out this agreement.

Acting in alignment with this agreement is our first priority in all CCE matters. All CCE participants are committed to live and work with one another in ways that create an increasing number of loving relationships of goodwill between members in our center and with the people we serve in the community. Our paid staff members, the members of our council of trustees, and CCE team program leaders agree to embody the tenets of this agreement.

Relational Interaction Agreement for CCE

In order to live out our shared principles and values, we, the staff, team leaders, and team members (volunteers) of the Center for Consciousness Education (CCE), commit to creating, implementing, and sustaining a culture of consideration, co-creation, and cooperative relationships. Therefore, we agree to uphold the following core beliefs and behaviors in our relationships with one another and in our relationships with those who are served by the activities of our center:

- **We know above all things that we are "love" and that the actions we take will always affect other people in our center and community**. Team members/leaders (volunteers) in our center agree to abide by our agreed upon CCE 10 Step Decision Making Process (Appendix E). All decisions will be made in alignment with this Agreement of Relational Interaction and the purpose, principles, and plans of our center.

- **We know that every person is of esteemed value to CCE.** We will always, and in all ways, assume that each person has good intentions in regard to their involvement and actions taken in the context of CCE activities. We claim that everyone is always working for the good of themselves and others. When things do not go as we have planned, we refrain from faultfinding, blaming one another, and talking negatively about people to others. We honor each other by dialoging about the situation to clarify the issue. We make the commitment to stay in the room with one another to co-create solutions that work to address the issue. If we are unable to come to a workable solution in one meeting, before leaving, we will schedule another meeting to continue creating workable solutions. We use the CCE 10 Step Decision Making Process to co-create and implement a solution.

- **We know that we are called to stay in "love" by seeking reconciliation through forgiveness when we experience difficulty in our relationships with one another.** We address conflict by meeting in person with each other as soon as possible. In the time between asking for a meeting and the actual meeting, we agree to hold one another in prayer and will not address or discuss conflict situations with others in person or in e-mails outside of that meeting. We agree with Gil Rendle's definition that, *conflict is the presence of two or more ideas in the same place at the same time.* Therefore, when conflict occurs, we will take the time necessary to listen to the ideas of everyone involved. We will then use our CCE 10 Step Decision Making Process to discern the next best step that we can take in order to live in alignment with the guiding documents of our center.

- **We know that we are a part of co-creating our relational and organizational experience of love and inclusivity.** When we experience relational separation, each person has a part in creating that experience. Therefore each individual will own their part and agree to work with others to create a solution that works to regain relational harmony. To create this harmony, we will honor and respect people by not interrupting them when they are sharing their ideas. We will not debate the validity of any idea shared. We will view all ideas as valid information to be used in our CCE 10 Step Decision Making Process.

- **We know nothing other than divine good in all situations and all people**. We take the responsibility to proactively own and share our individual thoughts and feelings about any situation, whether we consider them to be negative or positive. We do not withhold our truth. We share what is true for us without denigrating others. By being transparent and sharing our individual knowledge and perspectives, we then have access to the best information and wisdom upon which to base our decisions.

- **We know our paid and non-paid leaders serve to gather the collective wisdom of our center participants and make decisions in accordance with our guiding documents.** At all times our leaders will

be held accountable to show how they have made decisions and create policies and processes that are in alignment with the guiding documents of our center.

- **<u>We know God is our source and supply.</u>** In order
to implement the program plan as discerned by the
collective wisdom of the community, we trust that all
things are provided to meet our needs. Until the time,
talent, and funds are made available to us we go into the
silence and seek more guidance and direction from Spirit.
When resources are made available, our leaders will take
action to facilitate the co-creation and implementation of
our plans for the highest good of our community.

- **<u>We know the development of our community
involves the participation of people.</u>** All people
agree to participate in their willingness to be involved
and to the capacity of their current level of consciousness.
We welcome and recognize everyone's participation in
the growth of our community.

- **<u>We know there are many paths that lead to God.</u>**
We welcome everyone to our community and trust every
person's higher guidance to determine if CCE's path is
right for them. If CCE is no longer the path that is right
for someone, we lovingly let him or her go and keep a light
lit so that they may return when and if they so choose.

**<u>We know that the essential activity of our center is the
individual and collective growth in levels of consciousness and the capacity to embody the principles and practices of our spiritual community.</u>** Therefore, all paid staff
members are hired to be able to create learning opportunities that
equip team members (volunteers) and other center event attendees

to experience growth in consciousness and in the embodying of the principles and practices of our community.

- **We know God's grace in times when we slip back into acting in ways that are aligned with _a Me_Way culture of command, control, and blaming relationships**. When this occurs we will stop our conversation, ask for forgiveness, acknowledge the slip, and then shift back to dealing with the situation in alignment with our CCE culture of consideration, co-creation, and cooperative relationships. We will treat our slips as learning opportunities and teaching moments in which we are given the additional practice time to realign in love for and with one another.

Appendix E: 10 Step WeWay Decision Making Process

1. Clarify the issue.

2. Discern whether the decision is technical*, adaptive*, or both:

Characteristics of a *technical* decision:

- ❑ We have dealt with this issue before

- ❑ We know how to address the issue in a way that works in alignment with our guiding documents

- ❑ We have to comply with mandatory rules of law (city, state, federal, international)

- ❑ Requires no new information, input from others, or learning

- ❑ The task is already routinely done by someone or can easily be assigned to someone who can complete the task with little assistance

❏ Does not require that we create a new shared agreement

❏ Does not involve adaptive work; thus there is no need to do steps 3–10 of the 10 Step Process

Characteristics of an *adaptive* decision:

❏ A new issue is presented that we haven't dealt with before

❏ We have received new information that no longer allows us to deal with the issue in the same way as we have in the past

❏ What will work to address the issue in alignment with our shared agreements documents, isn't clear to us and we have a lot of different "I" perspectives about the issue (my "I" vs. your "I" feeling)

❏ Requires input from those who will be affected by the decision

❏ Requires new information or learning something new to deal with the issue (usually outside the current knowledge of the organization or relationship—"we" really don't know what the workable solution is)

❏ Solutions that we used in the past are no longer effective in addressing the issue

❏ Requires yielding one's personal "I" perspective and entering a co-creative, learning process so that together we can find a new "We" solution can be found

❑ Requires completing at least one 10 Step Process, if not several, to find a positive and constructive solution that works to sustain organizational/relational integrity for the relationship or the organization

The concepts of technical and adaptive decisions were coined by Ron Heifitz in his book Leading Without Easy Answers.

STEPS 3–10: *USED TO DEAL WITH ADAPTIVE DECISIONS*

3. Make a list of the persons who could be affected by any potential decision made on the issue:

A. Organization-wide decisions that will require inviting everyone to give their input:

1. Creating or modifying the guiding documents of the organization

2. Change of organization's location/facilities

3. Change in regular, ongoing events that involve the participation of large numbers of people in event preparation or attendance

B. All other decisions: Staff members, team leaders, and team members, whether paid or not paid, are held accountable to provide a rationale for their decisions/actions so that they are made in alignment with and in service to fulfilling the shared agreements of the relationship or the organization (our "We"). All people are free to be creative in addressing how things get done in their areas of responsibility and at the same time the relationship or organization is able to sustain its integrity.

4. Gather individual input of those listed in step three:

A. Use open-ended questions or descriptions of situations and ask people to individually write down their ideas and submit them without identification, or conduct individual interviews to receive input without discussion/debate with or judgment from others. Do not use multiple-choice survey questions unless the intention is to acquire only demographic information.

B. Compile a list of all the input by individuals.

5. Conduct a thematic analysis of the data to identify input where two or more ideas are in agreement (ideas that are the same or similar):

A. List all the ideas where two or more people give a similar or the same response.

B. Create a new list where ideas are ranked from most agreement to least agreement.

6. Check to see if each of the ideas on the ranked list (5B) are in alignment with the shared agreements of the relationship or organization (guiding documents, relational interaction agreement, etc.):

A. Ideas not in alignment are removed from the list by consent. Consent means we say yes to keeping an idea on the list, unless there are reasoned arguments or substantive objections presented that justify removing an idea from the list because they are not deemed to be in alignment with shared agreements.

B. Substantive evidence based on the guiding documents (not hearsay or personal preference) must be presented and consented to by all people present to remove an idea from the list.

7. **Brainstorm to co-create a solution to implement the idea found in first position on the ranked list.**

8. **Implement the solution created in step seven.**

9. **Evaluate progress.**

10. **Conduct another 10 Step Process when needed.**

About the Author

Wendy Foxworth is a captivating speaker, an effective development consultant, a highly regarded leader, workshop facilitator, mediator, **We**Way Relation-Shift coach and consultant for couples, work groups, and organizations. Her passion is to help people grow from self-centered to relational consciousness in the context of their relationships with others, personally and professionally. Wendy helps people learn how to embrace change as a positive opportunity to co-create a better world through relationships with others.

As a mediator, facilitator, and coach, she helps people create life-giving solutions to difficult situations, enabling people to co-create and sustain constructive and productive relationships. Wendy is soulful, passionate, and vibrant. She is dedicated to making life an enjoyable and enriching experience for herself and others.

Wendy is a former Christian minister, and is currently active as an independent business owner for Foxworth Coaching and Consulting Services, also serving as the director of The Center for Consciousness Education (previously the Center for Conscious Living), a nonprofit consciousness learning organization, in Albuquerque, New Mexico. Wendy has spent the last twenty-five years perfecting her skills as a speaker, teacher, facilitator, consultant, coach, and mediator. She has over thirty years' experience working with organizations of various sizes. Additionally, she has earned two bachelor degrees in education and theology and possesses a Master's degree in Managerial Leadership from John F. Kennedy University where she specialized in co-creating and sustaining learning communities.

She believes her effectiveness in providing services to people and organizations has been dependent on her understanding that *people who adapt well to changes are usually successful in accomplishing what they set out to do.* As a licensed trainer of **The Change Cycle®**, Wendy helps others understand how they can become successful changers themselves in order to make the shift from *Me*Ways to **We**Ways of relating.

Since all results happen through relationship, she recommends that employees, employers, and partners in all forms of relationship take this training so that they can more easily adapt to the changes that making a change in relational interaction patterning will require. Wendy's workshops and training programs focus on helping organizations and people grow in their ability to establish and succeed in fulfilling goals through forming respectful relationships, treating the planet with honor and care, and being profitable in sustainable ways for the greater good.

For more information on how you can get involved in co-creating a **We**Way world, call Wendy at 505-514-2024 or email her at wendyfoxworth@aol.com.